BOUNDARIES WITHOUT GUILT

How to Stop People-Pleasing, Set Firm Limits, and Take Back Your Power

Kim R. Toppin

BOUNDARIES WITHOUT GUILT

Published independently by Kim R. Toppin via Kindle Direct Publishing (KDP).

Printed in the United States of America. First Edition.

ISBN: 979-8-9940862-7-8 (Paperback)

DISCLAIMER

The content of this book is written for educational and informational purposes only. The insights, strategies, and exercises shared here are meant to support personal growth and understanding, but they are not a substitute for medical, psychological, legal, or financial advice.

Nothing in this book is intended to replace therapy, counseling, or clinical treatment. If you are experiencing mental health concerns, please consult a qualified healthcare professional. If you need legal or financial guidance, please consult a licensed professional in those areas.

The author has written this book with care and with the sincere hope that it will inform, encourage, and support you. Because every person's circumstances are different, the information provided should be applied in the way that best fits your situation using your own careful judgement. Readers are encouraged to use their own judgement.

The strategies offered here are tools, not guarantees. Your experience and results will be your own.

DEDICATION

For everyone who has ever swallowed a no

to keep someone else comfortable.

For the seekers, the givers, and the ones who stayed too long,

and everyone who decided, at last,

that they were worth protecting too.

TABLE OF CONTENTS

Introduction

PART ONE: Understanding People-Pleasing

Chapter 1: Why You Say Yes When You Mean No...............1
Chapter 2: The Cost of Keeping the Peace..............................6
Chapter 3: Where People-Pleasing Comes From...................10
Chapter 4: What You've Been Protecting Yourself From.....14
Chapter 5: The Permission You've Been Waiting For...........19

PART TWO: Setting Limits in Real Life

Chapter 6: Boundaries with Family.......................................25
Chapter 7: Boundaries at Work..32
Chapter 8: Boundaries in Friendships...................................39
Chapter 9: Boundaries in Romantic Relationships................47
Chapter 10: Boundaries with Toxic and Narcissistic People.55

PART THREE: Communicating Boundaries

Chapter 11: The Language of Limits.....................................65
Chapter 12: Having the Conversation....................................73
Chapter 13: When Guilt Shows Up.......................................82
Chapter 14: Handling Pushback...90
Chapter 15: Consequences That Mean Something................97

PART FOUR: Holding Your Ground

Chapter 16: When People Change, and When They Don't..106

Chapter 17: Self-Respect as a Practice................................114
Chapter 18: Staying Consistent...122
Chapter 19: When Your Limits Change You......................129
Chapter 20: Boundaries and Belonging..............................136

PART FIVE: Living Boundary-Forward

Chapter 21: The Generous Life..144
Chapter 22: Teaching Others Through Your Example........151
Chapter 23: When It's Hard...158
Chapter 24: Your Boundary Blueprint................................165
Chapter 25: You Are Allowed..172

Bonus Materials...180
Recommended Reading...185
A Final Note on Getting Help..187
About the Author..188

PART ONE

Understanding People-Pleasing

Chapter 1: Why You Say Yes When You Mean No

You know the moment. Someone makes a request, and before you have time to check in with yourself, the word yes is already out of your mouth. Not reluctantly. Not with conditions. A clean, automatic yes, delivered so smoothly it surprises even you.

And then, somewhere in the hours that follow, the resentment settles in. The quiet dread of what you have committed to. The exhaustion of knowing you have done it again. You ask yourself the familiar question with no good answer: why do I keep doing this?

This book begins with that question. Not with scripts and strategies. Those come later. It begins with the honest examination of why saying yes when you really mean no has become so automatic that it barely feels like a choice anymore.

It Was Never About Being Nice

The most common story people tell about their people-pleasing is that they do it because they are caring people who hate to see others disappointed and kindness matters to them.

That story is true as far as it goes, but it does not go far enough.

If your desire to people-please came purely from care, you would feel genuinely good after saying yes. You would feel warmth, generosity, and the satisfaction of having given something freely.

Instead, you often feel resentful, depleted, and quietly furious with yourself and the person who asked. Those are not feelings of generosity. They are the feelings of obligation. They come from giving something you did not freely choose to give because saying no felt more dangerous than saying yes.

Here is the truth most books on this topic will soften before they say it: people-pleasing is not primarily about caring for others. It is primarily about managing fear. The fear of disapproval. The fear of conflict. The fear of abandonment. The fear that if you do not give people what they want, something will break, someone will leave, and you will lose your place.

The care is real. But the care is not what is driving the yes. The fear is.

The Yes That Has a Price

There are two kinds of yes. The first comes from genuine desire, genuine availability, genuine care. You want to help. You have the capacity. You say yes and feel good about it. That yes costs you nothing, because it was freely chosen.

Then there is the other yes. The one you give when you are already depleted. When you have plans you did not mention because you knew they would be inconvenient. When you stay late at work for the third time this week because you cannot figure out how to stop. When you smile through something that hurts because naming it feels too risky. When you agree to something that you will spend the next week quietly resenting.

That yes has a price. Not always an obvious one, not a bill that arrives in the mail, but a cumulative one. It costs you time you did not have. Energy you needed for yourself. And, most significantly, the version of yourself that knows what it wants and believes it is allowed to want it.

That version of you is still there. It is just very quiet, because it learned early that speaking up causes problems.

Understanding this distinction is the foundation of everything in this book. The goal is not to say no more often. The goal is to say yes only when you mean it, and to be honest with yourself first when you do not.

What Fear Actually Sounds Like

People-pleasing fear does not usually announce itself as fear. It disguises itself as consideration, as practicality, as reading the room.

It sounds like:

It is not worth the argument.

They need me more than I need the afternoon.

I can handle it; it is not a big deal.

If I say no, they will think I am selfish.

I do not want to make things awkward.

It is just easier to say yes.

None of these sound like fear at first. They come across as reasonable, even responsible decisions. But underneath each one is the same quiet calculation: you believe the cost of saying no is higher than the cost of saying yes.

The calculation is wrong. The cost of an automatic yes, paid slowly and often unnoticed over months and years, is almost always higher than you realize. It slips past you because it does not show up all at once but builds quietly over time. No single yes breaks you; it is the accumulation that finally does.

The Moment Before the Yes

There is usually a moment, brief, sometimes almost imperceptible, between the request and your response. A moment in which you know what you actually want to say.

For most people-pleasers, that moment gets overridden almost immediately. The knowledge of what you actually want is there and then it is gone, replaced by the calculation of what will cause the least friction. The response happens before you have a real choice in it. Learning to notice that moment, to pause in it, to let it last long enough to actually inform your response, is one of the most fundamental skills this book will build. Not because you will always say no when you notice it. But because you cannot make a genuine choice from a place you cannot access.

The yes that comes from genuine desire is fundamentally different from the one that comes from fear. They can look identical from the outside. They feel completely different on the inside. Learning to tell them apart, in real time, in the middle of ordinary life, is one of the most important skills this book will build.

Why Change Feels So Hard

If people-pleasing is causing you harm, why do you keep doing it? Most people ask themselves this late at night, usually after agreeing to something they did not want to.

It is not a weakness. People-pleasing works, at least in the short term. It reduces conflict, keeps others comfortable, and brings approval. The problem is the cost over time.

Your nervous system learned this pattern for a reason. The automatic yes was a solution to a real problem at some point in your life. Nervous systems do not forget what kept them safe, so they keep running the same response long after the circumstances that required it have changed.

This is not a character flaw. It is part of being human, which is why changing this pattern takes more than deciding to do things differently. Your nervous system needs new evidence, gained through real experience, that the feared consequences of saying no are not what it believes them to be.

Real change comes from practice, step by step, in ways small enough to feel survivable and significant enough to matter.

Reflection Questions

1. Think of the last time you said yes when you wanted to say no. In the moment before you answered, did you know what you wanted to say? What happened to that knowing?
2. What does resentment feel like in your body after you have agreed to something you did not want? Where do you feel it, and how long does it last?
3. Is there a specific person or situations where the automatic yes shows up most? What is different about that context?
4. When you imagine saying no clearly, without apologizing or over-explaining, what is your first internal response?
5. What would change in your daily life this week if you said yes only when you meant it?

Your Chapter 1 Practice

This week, pay attention to the moment just before your yes. You do not need to change your answer yet. Your only task is to notice what happens in that space. Was there a split second where you knew what you wanted to say? What was it? What happened between that moment and your response?

Write down two or three of these moments. Not to judge yourself, but to see the pattern more clearly. Pay attention to what you felt, what you thought, and what you anticipated might happen if you answered differently. Most people-pleasing happens below conscious awareness. This week is about bringing it into view so you can begin to work with it.

Chapter 2: The Cost of Keeping the Peace

Keeping the peace sounds noble. Virtuous, even. You are the one who smooths things over, absorbs friction, and makes sure everyone gets along. You prevent arguments. You defuse tension. You keep the family dinner from becoming a confrontation and the work meeting from going sideways.

What nobody talks about is the actual cost. Not the occasional price of a single swallowed moment, but the cumulative cost of making it your job, year after year, to keep everyone around you undisturbed.

The Invisible Tax

Every time you keep the peace at your own expense, you pay a tax. It is invisible because no one sends you an invoice. But it compounds, and it is real.

You pay it in energy spent monitoring the room and adjusting yourself to manage other people's emotional states. You pay it in mental bandwidth used to rehearse what you will say, how they might respond, and how you will handle that response. You pay it in the emotional weight of what you absorb without naming: the comment that landed wrong, the dismissal you did not challenge, the moment that called for honesty but got compliance instead.

None of these costs are dramatic on their own. That is what makes them easy to dismiss. But over months and years, they add up to someone who is exhausted in ways they cannot fully explain, resentful in ways that feel disproportionate, and increasingly disconnected from what they actually want.

What Resentment Is Actually Telling You

Resentment has a bad reputation. It is treated as a character flaw, as evidence of pettiness or a failure to be generous. But resentment is not a flaw. It is a signal.

It is your emotional system flagging an unfair transaction. Something you gave without freely choosing to give. Something you absorbed that you should not have had to carry.

When resentment shows up, the question is not how do I get rid of this feeling. The question is: what produced it? What did I give that I did not want to give? What did I tolerate that I should have addressed?

Resentment points directly to your unset limits. It maps everything you have been swallowing in the name of keeping the peace. The goal is not to numb it. The goal is to address what is causing it.

The Performance of Fine

One of the most exhausting parts of keeping the peace is the performance that comes with it. Not just the swallowed no, but the smile that follows. I am fine when you are not. The warmth you generate on demand to reassure someone that everything is okay.

People-pleasers become expert performers. They can be hurt and appear fine. They can be running on empty and project warmth and capability. They can be furious and come across as easygoing.

This performance adds another layer of cost. It requires you to manage not just your actions, but your emotional presentation, keeping others comfortable regardless of what you actually feel.

Over time, it has a predictable effect: you stop knowing what you feel. Not because it disappeared, but because you have overridden it for so long that the signal becomes harder to hear.

Who Keeps the Peace, and Who Benefits

Here is a question worth sitting with: in the relationships where you do most of the peace-keeping, who actually benefits?

Typically, you benefit very little. You get to avoid the immediate discomfort of conflict, which is real, and feels like a benefit in the moment. But the person whose behavior prompted the conflict continues unchanged. The dynamic that requires peace-keeping continues unchanged. And you continue paying the invisible tax.

The person who benefits is the one whose behavior never has to change because someone else is always absorbing its cost.

This is not a comfortable realization. It does not mean the people in your life are deliberately exploiting you. Most of them are simply operating within a dynamic that works for them, largely unaware of what it costs you, because you have been hiding that cost very effectively.

But it does mean that the peace you are keeping is, in part, a peace that serves them more than it serves you.

The Limit You Have Not Set Yet

Under every act of peace-keeping is a limit that has not been set. Something you have chosen, consciously or not, to absorb rather than address. A behavior you have tolerated rather than named.

These unset limits accumulate, and they lead to one of two outcomes. The first is an explosion: everything you have swallowed comes out at once, disproportionate and confusing to everyone, including you. The second is an implosion: withdrawal, shutdown, the quiet decision to stop investing in a relationship that has cost you too much for too long.

Neither outcome is what you want. Both are the result of choosing, again and again, to absorb instead of address.

The alternative is not conflict for its own sake. It is honest communication before things reach a breaking point. It is addressing what is small and manageable instead of waiting until it is not. That is what limits are for.

Reflection Questions

1. What are you currently keeping the peace about? Name two or three situations or relationships where you are absorbing something you have not addressed.
2. What does your resentment map look like right now? Which situations or people appear most frequently on it?
3. Who benefits from the peace you keep? Is the cost shared fairly?
4. What are you performing? What emotional state are you projecting that does not match what you actually feel?
5. What would need to change for you to move from absorbing to addressing?

Your Chapter 2 Practice

This week, make a list of everything you are currently absorbing in the name of keeping the peace. Do not address it yet. Just make it visible. Write it down without editing for fairness or reasonableness. Simply name what is there.

Then look at the list. Notice how long it is. Notice how long some of these things have been there. That list is the shape of your unset limits. It is the raw material you will be working with going forward.

Chapter 3: Where People-Pleasing Comes From

People-pleasing does not arrive fully formed in adulthood. It is learned, shaped by early experiences and relationships that taught you, at a level deeper than words, how people responded when you expressed your needs and when you stayed quiet.

Understanding where it came from does not excuse the work of changing it. But it does something important: it helps you stop treating it as a character flaw and start seeing it as a strategy. One that made sense once but has outlived its usefulness.

The Early Learning

Most people-pleasing has roots in childhood. Not always in dramatic trauma, though sometimes that. More often in the steady accumulation of messages about what was safe and what was not.

Children are highly attuned to their environments. They are wired to read the adults around them and adjust, because their survival depends on those adults' care and approval. When a child learns that having needs leads to withdrawal, anger, or disappointment, they begin to minimize those needs.

When expressing an opinion causes conflict, they suppress it. When showing anger leads to punishment, they hide it. When being inconvenient costs them warmth and attention, they learn to be agreeable above all else.

None of this is a conscious decision. It is an adaptation. The child becomes whoever they need to be to maintain safety and connection in their environment. And the strategy works in the short term, in that context. The problem is that the brain encodes it as a general rule rather than a situational one.

The Messages That Installed It

Love was conditional on compliance. Approval came when you were agreeable and undemanding. It withdrew when you were not.

Conflict was dangerous. Arguments escalated in ways that felt unpredictable or threatening. Keeping the peace became a survival skill, not just a preference.

Your needs were treated as burdens. Asking for something brought sighs, complaints, or reminders of everything the adults were already managing. You learned to ask less, and eventually to stop asking.

Self-sacrifice was modeled and praised. The adults around you gave until they collapsed and were celebrated for it. Putting yourself first was framed as selfish.

Your feelings were dismissed. You were told you were too sensitive, that you were overreacting, that you should think about how your emotions affected others. You learned your emotional experience was less important.

You absorbed these messages not as lessons, but as truths. They became part of how you understand the world and your place in it. They became the operating system underneath every interaction.

When It Was the Right Strategy

This is the part that gets left out of most conversations about people-pleasing: it was the right strategy at the time.

In a home where conflict was genuinely dangerous, learning to prevent it from escalating was intelligent. In a relationship where love was conditional on compliance, becoming compliant was adaptive. In an environment where your needs produced resentment, minimizing them was a reasonable response to real conditions.

You did not develop people-pleasing because you were weak or foolish. You developed it because you were paying attention. Because you were doing the best possible thing with the information and resources you had at the time.

The problem is not that you learned it. The problem is that you are still running that strategy in environments that do not require it. That you are protecting yourself from dangers that are no longer present, at the cost of genuine living.

Other Sources of People-Pleasing

Not all people-pleasing begins in childhood. It can also develop through adult experiences.

A romantic relationship or close friendship that rewarded compliance and punished assertiveness can install these patterns just as deeply. If you spent time with someone who responded to your needs with anger, withdrawal, or manipulation, you learned your needs were the problem.

Many cultures, communities, and religious traditions reinforce the same message: that self-sacrifice is a virtue, putting others first is moral, and having limits is selfish. These ideas become so pervasive that they feel invisible.

Women, in particular, are socialized to prioritize others' comfort, to be accommodating and agreeable, and to treat self-advocacy as aggression. These expectations are reinforced constantly through language, media, and the different responses people receive when they express needs or set limits.

For some people, people-pleasing is directly tied to trauma. The fawning response, alongside fight, flight, and freeze, is a survival strategy that appeases a threat by prioritizing someone else's needs over your own. It is effective in real danger but can become a default response long after the danger has passed.

Reflection Questions

1. What early messages did you receive about having needs or expressing disagreement? Where do you think your people-pleasing begins?
2. Was there a specific relationship, in childhood or adulthood, that reinforced this pattern most? What did that relationship teach you?
3. What was the people-pleasing strategy originally protecting you from? Was that something genuinely dangerous, or did it feel dangerous at the time?
4. Are the conditions that made people-pleasing necessary still present in your life? Or are you still using an old strategy in a new environment?
5. What would you say to the younger version of yourself who developed this pattern? What do you know now that they did not know then?

Your Chapter 3 Practice

This week, write a brief history of your people-pleasing. Not a clinical analysis, but a story. Where did it start? Who was involved? What were you protecting yourself from? What did it cost you then, and what is it costing you now?

You are not writing this to blame anyone. You are writing it to understand. Understanding is the first step toward choosing differently. And compassion for the version of you who developed this pattern, the one who was trying to survive, is the foundation for everything that comes next.

Chapter 4: What You Have Been Protecting Yourself From

Every people-pleasing behavior is a form of protection. Not a random habit, not a personality trait you were born with, but a deliberate, if unconscious, shield against something that felt threatening.

This chapter asks you to look directly at what you have been protecting yourself from. Not to dismiss the fear, because it came from something real, but to examine whether the protection is still necessary and what it is costing you to keep it in place.

The Fear of Rejection

Underneath much people-pleasing is the fear that if you disappoint someone, they will leave. That if you say no, you will lose them. That your place in a relationship, a family, a friendship, or a workplace is contingent on your continued agreeableness.

This fear often has a specific origin: a relationship or environment where approval was conditional, where love, acceptance, or belonging seemed to disappear whenever you were inconvenient. The fear made sense then. But over time, it begins to generalize, extending to relationships where it no longer belongs and to people who are not actually going to leave simply because you disappoint them.

A useful question is: is this person, in this situation, actually likely to leave if I disappoint them? Not based on your history with someone else, but on the evidence you have about this person.

The Fear of Conflict

For some people-pleasers, it is not the outcome of conflict they avoid, but the experience itself. The raised voices, the tension, the feeling of being at odds with someone. This fear is particularly common in people who grew up in homes where conflict was volatile or unpredictable.

When conflict was genuinely unsafe, avoiding it was intelligent. But the nervous system does not automatically distinguish between the conflict that was dangerous and the ordinary friction of honest communication. It treats them the same way, as threats to be neutralized.

What this means in practice is that even a mild disagreement can trigger a fear response that is sized for a much more dangerous situation. The body is reacting to the past. The present situation is rarely as dangerous as the nervous system believes.

The Fear of Being Too Much

Many people-pleasers carry a deep, often wordless belief that their real self, with their needs, opinions, and edges, is too much. Too demanding. Too difficult. Too much to ask someone to love.

This belief usually has a specific origin: repeated messages that their natural expression was inconvenient or unwelcome, that they needed to be smaller, quieter, less.

People-pleasing becomes a way of managing that fear. If you make yourself small enough, agreeable enough, useful enough, maybe you will not be too much. Maybe you will finally be acceptable.

The problem is that it never resolves the fear. You can spend years shrinking yourself and still feel like too much, because the belief was never based on reality. It was based on someone else's limitations.

The Fear of Guilt

Some people-pleasers are not primarily afraid of others' reactions. They are afraid of how they will feel if they disappoint someone.

The guilt is what they are avoiding. The experience of having let someone down, of being the cause of someone's unhappiness, of being a bad person.

This is especially common in people with strong empathy, those who feel others' emotional states acutely and find it genuinely painful to be the source of someone's distress, even when that distress is appropriate.

The problem is that when you organize your behavior around avoiding guilt, you give other people enormous power over you without them having to do anything. All they have to do is appear unhappy, and you will adjust.

What the Protection Has Cost You

Each of these fears is real. Each of the protections built around them made sense at some point. But protection always has a cost, and the cost of people-pleasing is significant.

You have not been fully known by the people in your life, because the version of you they know has been carefully managed.

You have accumulated resentment from giving what you did not freely choose to give.

You have exhausted yourself monitoring and managing others' emotional states.

You have missed opportunities for genuine connection, for honest communication, for the things you actually wanted, because the fear made them feel too risky.

You have taught the people around you that your limits do not exist, which means they have never had to learn to respect them.

And you have quietly communicated to yourself, through years of overriding your own needs, that your needs do not matter enough to protect. That you do not matter enough to protect.

When the Fear Is Worth Examining

Not all fear is irrational. Some situations genuinely warrant caution. Some relationships do require careful handling. Some conflicts are not worth having.

The question to ask is: is this an accurate assessment of the current situation, or a response to a past situation that no longer applies?

Is this person actually likely to leave if you disappoint them, or are you applying the lesson of a different relationship?

Is this conflict truly dangerous, or does it just feel the way conflict used to feel?

Is your real self actually too much, or did someone with their own limitations teach you that when you were too young to question it?

The answers may not make the fear disappear, but they can create space between the fear and the automatic behavior it produces. And that space is where choice lives.

Reflection Questions

Which of these fears resonates most strongly with you? What does it feel like when it is activated?

Where did that fear come from? Can you trace it to a specific relationship or experience?

Is this fear an accurate reflection of your current life, or a holdover from something that no longer applies?

What has this protection cost you? Be specific. What have you missed, lost, or given up because of it?

What would you need to believe about yourself, or about the people in your life, for this fear to lose some of its power?

Your Chapter 4 Practice

This week, when you notice yourself people-pleasing, pause and ask: what am I afraid will happen if I do not? Name the fear specifically. Not something bad, but what exactly. Who does what? What is lost?

Then ask: is that actually likely to happen in this situation with this person?

You do not need to act differently yet. Just begin examining the fear instead of automatically responding to it. Naming a fear and looking at it directly starts to reduce its power, slowly but genuinely.

Chapter 5: The Permission You Have Been Waiting For

Many people who struggle with people-pleasing are waiting for permission, without fully realizing it.

Permission to have limits. To say no. To take up space, to have needs, to show up fully and honestly without apologizing for the inconvenience.

You have read the books and heard the advice. You know, intellectually, that you have the right to protect yourself. But somewhere deeper, you are still waiting for someone, a parent, a partner, a therapist, a voice outside you, to say it is truly okay.

This chapter offers that permission. Not because you need it from me, you do not, and we will get to that, but because sometimes it helps to hear it stated plainly before the work begins.

You Are Allowed

You are allowed to have needs.

You are allowed to say no.

You are allowed to be tired, overwhelmed, and at capacity.

You are allowed to disappoint people.

You are allowed to change your mind.

You are allowed to want things such as time, space, recognition, and reciprocity.

You are allowed to set a limit with someone you love and still love them.

You are allowed to protect yourself from being hurt, even by people whose intentions are good.

You are allowed to leave situations that consistently harm you.

You are allowed to prioritize your own wellbeing. That does not make you selfish, ungrateful, or a bad person.

None of this requires a particular set of circumstances. None of it requires that you first prove you have given enough, sacrificed enough, been accommodating enough. It applies to you now, as you are, in the life you are actually living.

Why External Permission Does Not Stick

Here is the difficult truth about external permission: it does not last.

You can be told you are allowed, by a therapist, a book, or a friend who loves you, and feel it deeply in the moment. Then the moment passes, and the old voice returns. The one that says you are being selfish, that you are too sensitive, that a truly good person would not need to have this conversation because they would simply give without being asked.

External permission does not override that voice because the voice is not responding to information. It is responding to a belief, a deep, pre-verbal conviction about your worth and your right to take up space. Beliefs do not change from new information. They change through new experiences.

The permission that lasts is built through action. Through saying no and surviving. Through disappointing someone and seeing that the relationship holds. Through setting a limit and discovering that the feared consequences either do not happen or are manageable when they do.

Words can point the way. But real permission comes from what you do. From saying no and seeing that nothing catastrophic happens. From disappointing someone and realizing the relationship can withstand it. From setting a limit and discovering you can handle the outcome.

The Difference Between Permission and Selfishness

The fear that stops many people-pleasers from claiming permission is the fear of becoming selfish. If I start saying no, will I stop caring about others? If I prioritize my needs, will I lose my compassion?

Here is the distinction: selfishness is the excessive prioritization of your needs at the expense of others. Limits are the recognition that your needs exist and matter, not more than others, but not less.

I come first; you do not matter is selfishness.

I matter too is a limit.

These are not the same. And someone who has spent years putting themselves last is in very little danger of suddenly swinging to the opposite extreme. This work is not about caring less about others. It is about including yourself in that care.

What This Work Will Actually Require

Before moving into the practical work ahead, it is worth being clear about what this will require.

It will require discomfort. These patterns are old and deeply wired. Changing them will feel wrong at first, not morally wrong, but unfamiliar and activating. Your nervous system will protest. The guilt will show up. The old voice may get louder before it quiets.

It will require honesty, especially with yourself, about what you feel, what you want, and what you have been tolerating. The managed version of you is practiced and convincing. Seeing through it takes effort.

It will require patience. This is not something you read once and feel transformed. It unfolds over time, through small choices that accumulate into a different way of being.

And it will require compassion. Toward yourself. Toward the version of you who developed these patterns for understandable reasons. And toward the imperfect process of changing them.

You already have what you need to begin. You have been doing it simply by reading this far.

Reflection Questions

1. What specific permission have you been waiting for? What is something you want to do or stop doing but have not fully allowed yourself?
2. Where does the voice come from that tells you that you are not allowed? Whose voice is it, really?
3. What is the difference, in your own experience, between a time you were genuinely generous and a time you gave out of obligation? How did each feel?
4. What are you most afraid will happen if you start claiming your permission to set limits? Is that fear based on what is happening now, or on something from your past?
5. What would the most self-respecting version of yourself do differently in your life right now, today, this week?

Your Chapter 5 Practice

This week, do one thing that the self-respecting version of yourself would do. Not the hardest thing. The smallest true thing. Something you have been avoiding because it felt too risky or too selfish or too much.

It might be as small as not answering a text you feel obligated to answer immediately. Leaving a situation when you are ready to leave, rather than when everyone else is. Saying I need a few minutes before responding to a request.

Do it. Notice what happens. The world will almost certainly not end. And you will have your first small piece of evidence that claiming your permission is survivable.

PART TWO

Setting Limits in Real Life

Chapter 6: Boundaries with Family

Some limits are difficult. Family limits feel impossible.

With a stranger, you can walk away. With a coworker, you can keep it professional. But family? They were there at the beginning. They know where you came from, what shaped you, and which buttons were installed before you even understood what limits were.

That is what makes this the hardest place to start. And that is exactly why it matters. If you can hold a limit with the people who have the most practice getting around them, you can hold one anywhere.

Why Family Limits Feel Different

When you say no to a friend, it might sting. When you say no to a family member, it can feel like you are rejecting the entire relationship. Betraying the people who raised you. Being ungrateful for everything they have done.

That feeling is not an accident. Many family systems, especially dysfunctional ones, operate on the unspoken rule that love means unlimited access. That closeness means you do not protect yourself. That loyalty means you absorb whatever is handed to you without complaint.

You were likely never taught that you can love someone and still say no to them. That you can honor your family and still protect yourself. That you can be a good daughter, son, sibling, or cousin and still have needs that matter.

You can. All of that is true at once. Love and limits are not opposites. In healthy relationships, they coexist. The work here is learning to hold both.

The Myths You Were Taught

Myth One: You owe them. You did not ask to be born. Your parents chose to have you, and raising a child is not a lifelong debt. Healthy parents give because they love, and not because they want to collect later. If someone reminds you of what they have done as a reason you must comply, that is not love. That is leverage.

Myth Two: They mean well. Intentions matter, but they do not erase impact. Someone can mean well yet cross your boundaries, dismiss your feelings, and leave you feeling worse after every interaction. Good intentions do not give anyone an unlimited license to hurt you.

Myth Three: Blood is thicker than water. This phrase is often used to guilt people into tolerating behavior they would never accept from anyone else. Shared DNA is not a waiver for basic respect.

Myth Four: They will never change, so why bother. Setting a limit is not about changing them. It is about changing what you will accept.

Common Family Violations Worth Naming

Learning to recognize what is actually a violation, rather than normal friction, is the first step.

Uninvited opinions about your life. Your weight, relationships, parenting, career, finances. Family members who treat your life as open for commentary.

Showing up unannounced. Your home is your space, not an extension of theirs.

Sharing your personal information without permission. The person who tells everyone your business.

Guilting you for not doing enough. No matter what you give, it is never quite right.

Using your children as leverage. Comments designed to override your comfort and your limits.

Treating your no as a negotiation. When your answer is met with pressure, persistence, and guilt until you give in.

Real-Life Script: The Holiday Pressure

Here is a common scenario: you decide not to attend a gathering, or to leave early, and the response is pressure.

They say: You never make time for this family. Your grandmother is getting older. You are going to regret this. We all make sacrifices. What is so important that you cannot be here?

What most people do: over-explain, justify, apologize, and eventually give in.

What you can say instead: I understand you are disappointed. I will not be able to make it this year.

That is enough. You do not owe them a reason good enough to satisfy them, because there is not one. No reason will be accepted as sufficient if they have already decided you are wrong for declining. The explanation is not the problem. Your no is the problem. And no explanation fixes that.

If they push: I have already made my decision. I hope everyone has a good time.

If they keep pushing: I am going to end this conversation now. We can talk another time.

Then do exactly that.

More Scripts for Common Family Situations

When They Give Unsolicited Opinions About Your Life

They say: You should lose some weight before the reunion. Or: I don't understand why you are still at that job. Or: Are you sure you want to raise your kids that way?

You can say:

I'm good with how things are.

I didn't ask for input on that.

That's not something I need advice on.

I've got it handled.

What's going on with you?

You do not have to argue, explain, or defend your choices. Redirect the conversation, or let the silence sit.

When They Share Your Personal Business

You find out a family member has shared your divorce, finances, health, or relationship with others. That is a violation, and it is worth addressing directly.

You can say: I found out you shared information about my situation with other family members. That was not yours to share. Going forward, what I tell you stays between us. If it happens again, I will be more careful about what I share with you.

Calm. Direct. No dramatics. Then follow through. If it continues, share less.

When They Drop By Unannounced

At the door: Hey, this isn't a good time. Can we plan something for next week?

If it keeps happening: I've noticed you've been stopping by without calling first. I need you to check in before coming over. I'm not always available, and I want to be present when we spend time together. Text or call, and I'll let you know what works.

If they make it dramatic: I'm not rejecting you. I'm asking for a heads-up. That's reasonable.

When It Is a Parent

Parent-child limits deserve their own conversation because the power dynamic runs deep. You spent your childhood needing them, and that wiring does not simply disappear.

What matters here is this: becoming an adult means the relationship is supposed to change. You are no longer someone who needs their guidance and approval for every decision. You are a full human being with the right to run your own life, even if they disagree.

That transition is harder when parents have not made it with you. Some stay stuck in the role of authority long past the point where it fits. Setting limits with them is not disrespect. It is growing up, even if it happens later.

Script for recurring criticism from a parent: Mom or Dad, I love you, and I want a good relationship with you. But when you comment on this, it hurts. I'm asking you to stop. If it continues, I will need to change how much time we spend together, because I want our time to feel good, not draining.

This is a limit with a consequence, and it is honest. You are not threatening them. You are being clear about what will happen if the dynamic does not change.

On Guilt

Here is what no one tells you about family limits: enforcing them feels terrible at first, even when you did nothing wrong.

You hold the limit and the guilt shows up. Maybe I should have just gone. Maybe I am being selfish. Maybe they are right.

This is not your conscience. It is conditioning. Years of being taught that your no is a problem, that your needs are inconvenient, that keeping the peace is your job. All of that surfaces the moment you push back.

The guilt is the old rule trying to stay in place. It does not mean you did something wrong. It means you did something new. Sit with it. Breathe through it. Do not go back and apologize for protecting yourself.

A Note on Estrangement

Sometimes the limit that serves you best is distance, significant, extended, or permanent. Estrangement from family is one of the most stigmatized decisions a person can make, and one of the most misunderstood.

People assume it is always extreme. That something catastrophic must have happened. Or that the person who stepped back is the problem: cold, unforgiving, difficult.

What they do not see are the years of smaller attempts. The conversations that went nowhere. The limits that were set and repeatedly crossed. The relationships that left someone emptier each time.

Estrangement is not failure. Sometimes it is the only limit left to set, the one that finally holds.

If you are considering it, you do not owe anyone an explanation. You do not have to justify protecting your peace. You are not required to maintain a relationship that consistently harms you simply because the person causing the harm shares your bloodline.

Reflection Questions

1. Which family member is hardest for you to say no to? What do you fear will happen if you do?
2. Think of a time you agreed to something with a family member purely out of guilt. How did you feel before, during, and after?
3. What is one limit you have been wanting to set with a family member but have not? What has stopped you?
4. What would you tell a close friend who described your exact situation? Would your advice to them be different from what you tell yourself?
5. What would change in your family relationships if they knew your no meant no and it stayed no?

Your Chapter 6 Practice

This week, identify one small limit to set or hold with a family member. It does not have to be the biggest one. It can be as simple as not answering a call you always feel obligated to answer, or redirecting a conversation that consistently drains you. goes somewhere draining.

Notice what happens inside you when you hold it. Notice whether they push back. Notice how you feel the next day.

You do not have to announce a limit for it to be real. You just have to hold the limit.

Chapter 7: Boundaries at Work

You spend more waking hours at work than almost anywhere else in your life. This means what happens at work matters more than most people admit: who gets credit, who absorbs extra work, who gets interrupted, and who stays late while others go home

People-pleasers often struggle most at work. The professional environment is built on hierarchy, performance, and the need to be liked and valued. The workplace can quickly become a perfect storm for someone who has spent years believing their worth depends on being agreeable and accommodating.

You stay late because you do not want to seem uncommitted. You take on extra projects because you do not want to disappoint your manager or your team. You let the credit for your work get absorbed by someone louder because confrontation feels too risky. You smile through condescension because the alternative feels worse.

This chapter is about stopping those patterns. Professionally, effectively, and without creating unnecessary conflict.

Why Work Limits Are Especially Hard

Workplace limits feel harder than personal ones because the consequences feel real and immediate.

Family limits often carry the fear of guilt or rejection. Workplace limits carry the risk of something more concrete, like losing your job, being passed over for a promotion, or gaining a reputation as being difficult.

These fears are not irrational, and they are powerful enough to keep people tolerating situations they know are not acceptable.

People who never push back at work are rarely rewarded for it. They are given more work, less respect, and often less pay. Over time, they communicate that they will accept whatever is handed to them.

The goal is not to become difficult. The goal is to know your value, communicate clearly, and stop absorbing situations that are not acceptable.

Common Workplace Violations Worth Naming

After-hours contact expectations. Being texted or emailed at night and on weekends with the expectation that you will respond immediately, even when it is not urgent, and you are not required to be available on weekends.

Scope creep and invisible overload. Your role gradually expands without a corresponding increase in pay, title, or *recognition. You say yes to one extra thing, then another, until your responsibilities no longer resemble what you were hired to do.

Credit theft. Your ideas are presented by someone else. Your work is folded into group deliverables without acknowledgment. Your insights are repeated in meetings as if they were someone else's.

Disrespectful communication. Being spoken to dismissively, talked over in meetings, interrupted repeatedly, or addressed with a tone that would not be acceptable outside of work.

Being volunteered without consent. Someone else is committing your time without asking first.

Emotional labor expectations. Being expected to manage others' moods, smooth over conflicts that are not yours, absorb a manager's stress, or regulate the emotional tone of the team on top of doing your actual job.

What You Are Actually Allowed To Do

A lot of people assume that at work, you have to take what is given, that pushing back puts you at risk, and that having limits makes you a problem employee.

That is not true. You are allowed to decline non-urgent requests outside of working hours. You are allowed to ask for clarity on scope before agreeing to additional work. You are allowed to name your contributions in meetings. You are allowed to push back professionally when communication is disrespectful. You are allowed to ask for a conversation about workload, compensation, or expectations. You are allowed to say I need to check my capacity before I commit.

None of these make you a difficult person. They make you someone who takes your professional role seriously, including the sustainability of your work.

Scripts for Common Workplace Situations

When You Are Asked to Take On More Than You Can Handle

The setup: your manager adds another project without asking about your capacity.

I want to make sure I can do this well. I currently have these projects with these deadlines. If I take this on, something will need to shift. Can we talk about priorities?

This makes your workload visible. It shows that you are not an unlimited resource. It places the prioritization decision where it belongs.

If your manager insists that everything must be done:

I can do that, but I want to be transparent. Something will likely be delayed or lower quality. I want you to know that so we can decide together where the tradeoff happens.

When Someone Takes Credit for Your Work

This happens more often than it should. Address it quickly and calmly.

In the moment: I want to add some context since I developed that approach. The thinking behind it was…

After the meeting: I noticed my work on this project was presented without attribution. I do not think that was intentional, but visibility for my contributions matters to me. Going forward, I would appreciate being credited when my work is referenced.

If it continues, document it and consider involving a manager or HR.

When You Are Contacted After Hours

Just a heads-up. I do not monitor work messages after this time unless something is urgent. I will respond in the morning.

If a manager raises expectations:

I want to make sure I am fully present during working hours. I am more effective when I have clear off-hours. Is there a specific concern we should address?

When You Are Spoken to Disrespectfully

In the moment: I would like to finish my point.

After a pattern develops: I want to address something directly. When I am interrupted or spoken to that way, it affects my ability to contribute. I would rather address it now than let it build.

If it continues and involves a supervisor, document specific instances and escalate appropriately.

When a Colleague Volunteers Your Time Without Asking

To the colleague: I would appreciate a heads-up before my name is offered. I am happy to help when I can, but I need to know my capacity before I commit.

To the person sent to you: I want to help if I can. Let me check my schedule and get back to you.

The Overachiever Trap

There is a version of people-pleasing at work that looks like success. The person who works the longest hours, takes on the most, never says no, and always delivers gets praised as a team player.

Over time, that person burns out. They realize they have been doing two people's jobs for one person's pay. They get passed over for promotion because they made themselves indispensable in their current role instead of positioning themselves to grow.

The overachiever trap is real. The way out is recognizing that your value does not come from being endlessly available. Saying yes to everything is not the same as being excellent.

Excellence requires protecting the time and energy needed to do your work well.

A Word on Difficult Supervises

Some situations involve managers who are genuinely difficult. The supervisor who takes credit. The supervisor who plays favorites. The manager who leads through intimidation.

Setting personal limits is still worth doing, but it will not fix a structural problem. That requires deciding whether to address it formally, work around it, or leave the environment.

No limit you set will change someone else's character. You can control what you accept, what you document, and what you do next.

What You Are Actually Allowed To Do at Work

Many high-performing people-pleasers often fall into the trap of becoming indispensable in their current role. They absorb extra work, say yes to everything, and become the person no one worries about.

They are praised but not promoted, relied on but not rewarded. The organization learns that high-performing people-pleasers will accept whatever is handed to them, making it easier to maintain that dynamic than to change it.

Saying no at work is not a career risk when it is done professionally and strategically. It signals that you understand the value of your time and manage it accordingly. It is not a liability; it is leadership.

Reflection Questions

Where at work do you say yes when you mean no? What do you fear will happen if you say no?

Think of a time your work was overlooked. How did you respond? How do you wish you had responded?

Do you check work messages after hours? Is it required, or do you feel obligated to?

What workplace pattern are you tolerating that you would not accept in a personal relationship?

What would change if people knew your no meant no and that you were at capacity?

Your Chapter 7 Practice

This week, identify one place at work where you have been overextending yourself without acknowledgment or compensation. Examples of this might include answering messages after hours, taking on extra work, or letting credit theft go unreported.

Choose one small action. Respond to the next after-hours message in the morning. Flag your workload in your next check-in. Name your contribution in your next meeting.

You do not have to overhaul everything this week. You only need to practice showing up as someone who knows the*ir worth. Over time, that practice becomes who you are at work.

effectively, and without burning anything down.

Chapter 8: Boundaries in Friendships

Friendships are supposed to be the relationships you get to choose in life. Unlike family, you were not born into these relationships, and are not obligated by a paycheck. Friendship is voluntary, which makes it a clear test of what you believe you deserve in a relationship.

And yet, some of the most persistent people-pleasing happens within friendships. The friend you always show up for who rarely shows up for you. The friend who calls only in crisis and disappears when things are good. As well as the friend whose problems always take center stage while yours wait in the wings.

You keep those friendships out of loyalty, history, guilt, or the fear that if you pull back, you will end up alone. So, you give more than you receive, tolerate more than you should, and tell yourself this is just what good friends do.

This chapter is about being honest with yourself about what your friendships are actually costing you, in time, energy, and emotional impact, and what you have the right to change.

The Baseline That Matters

Healthy friendships are not perfectly transactional. You do not keep score down to the last coffee or favor, but there is a baseline of reciprocity that matters, a sense that both people are investing, both are showing up, and both lives are visible in the relationship.

When that balance shifts significantly and remains that way, it stops being a friendship and becomes something else. It turns into a dynamic where one person gives and the other takes, and the giver, usually the people pleaser, continues to give because they have come to believe that is what caring looks like.

It is not. Caring about someone does not mean accepting a one-sided relationship.

Signs a Friendship Has Become One-Sided

You always initiate. If you stopped reaching out, the friendship would go quiet, and you know it.

Your problems get a fraction of the airtime. Conversations consistently circle back to their life, their stress, their needs. When you try to share something difficult, it gets acknowledged briefly and redirected.

You adjust for them but they don't adjust for you. You change plans, accommodate their schedule, make exceptions. When you need flexibility, it is rarely returned.

You feel drained after spending time with them. Not just tired, but depleted. Like you gave something and came back with less than you started with.

You filter yourself around them, holding back what you would normally share because you already know how it will land, with judgment, one-upmanship, or a shift back to them.

They are only available when things are good for them. In your hard moments, they are vague, busy, or missing entirely.

You feel guilty when you do not meet their expectations. When they react with disappointment or pull away after you set a limit, you take responsibility for how they feel.

The Three Types of Draining Friends

The Crisis Friend. Everything is always urgent with this person. Their life is in a constant state of emergency, and each crisis pulls you in for advice, support, practical help, and emotional labor. You are always on call.

What is exhausting is not caring about someone in a real crisis. It is becoming the constant support system for someone whose crises never end and whose situation never changes. If you stepped back, they would find someone else to take your place. That is not cold, it is honest. It also means your constant availability is not helping them move forward; it is allowing the pattern to continue.

The Competitor Friend. This friendship has an undercurrent of competition that never quite surfaced into a real conversation. When something good happens to you, they find a way to match it or minimize it. When something hard happens to you, they have a story that is harder. Your wins make them uncomfortable. Your losses make them feel better, though they would never say so.

Friendship should feel safe enough to celebrate and grieve openly. If you are editing your good news and your bad news to manage someone else's reaction, that is not friendship. It is performance.

The Disappearing Act Friend. This person is wonderful when they are present: warm, fun, genuinely connected. But their availability is entirely on their terms. They surface when they want company, go quiet when they are busy or happy, and reappear expecting to pick up exactly where things left off without acknowledging the gap.

You have probably made more excuses for this person than you realize. They are just bad at keeping in touch. They have a lot going on. That is just how they are.

Maybe. But you deserve friends who show up with some consistency. Not perfectly, but enough that you do not feel like an option.

What You Are Allowed to Want from a Friendship

This sounds obvious but it is not easy for people-pleasers. You are allowed to have standards for your friendships. You are allowed to want:

A friend who initiates sometimes, not just responds.

Space to talk about your own life without redirecting back to theirs.

Someone who shows up when things are hard for you, not just when they need something.

A friendship where you do not feel worse about yourself after spending time together.

The ability to say no without it threatening the entire relationship.

A friend who can handle your honesty and offer theirs in return.

Wanting those things does not make you demanding. It makes you someone who understands what friendship is meant to be and what it actually looks like.

Scripts for Friendship Situations

When You Need to Address the Imbalance

I want to talk to you about something because I value this friendship. I have noticed lately that I am usually the one reaching out, and when we talk, I feel like my concerns does not get as much space as yours. I am not saying that to be critical. I just need the friendship to feel more balanced. Is that something you are open to talking about?

What happens next tells you a lot. A friend who cares will hear it and engage. A friend who does not will make it about your sensitivity or turn it into a grievance against you. Either response is information.

When You Need to Say No to a Request

I cannot make that work. I hope it goes well.

That is not something I am able to take on right now.

I am going to sit this one out.

You do not owe a reason. A reason invites negotiation. A warm, simple no is complete.

If they push: I understand you are disappointed. My answer is still no.

When You Need to Reduce Contact Without a Big Conversation

Not every friendship that has run its course needs a formal conversation about ending. Sometimes the most honest thing is a gradual, quiet pulling back.

Begin to respond more slowly, mention being busy when plans are suggested, stop initiating, and allow the friendship to settle at its natural level.

This is not ghosting. Ghosting is disappearing without explanation from someone who has reasonable cause to expect more from you. Quietly reducing investment in a friendship that has been draining you is not the same thing.

When a Friend Crosses a Specific Line

For the confidence violation: I found out you mentioned what I told you about this situation to other people. That was not okay with me. What I share with you, I expect to stay between us. If that is not something you can do, I will need to be more careful about what I share.

For the cutting remark: That landed as a dig, even if it was not meant that way. I want to be able to tell you when something does not feel good.

For chronic cancellation: I have noticed plans with you fall through a lot. I do not want to keep making plans that do not happen. Can we talk about what is going on?

When a Friendship Has to End

Some friendships end because they have run their natural course. You grew in different directions, life circumstances changed, and the thing that held you together is gone. That kind of ending is sad but clean.

Other friendships end because the dynamic was never healthy, and you finally stopped pretending it was. Those endings are harder because they come with grief, not just for the friendship but for the version of yourself that kept accepting less than you deserved.

You do not owe anyone a formal breakup speech for a friendship. But if someone asks directly why you have pulled back, you can be honest without being cruel:

I have realized this friendship has not been feeling good for me for a while. I wish you well, but I am not in a place to continue it.

Then hold the line. Do not get pulled back in by their reaction, their guilt trips, or the fear of being too harsh. The experience of that friendship is already clear, and there is no need to justify protecting yourself from more of it.

A Note on Loneliness

The fear beneath all of this is that if you set limits in friendships, pull back from draining ones, and refuse one-sided dynamics, you will be left alone.

That fear is real and worth naming. Loneliness is painful, and for people-pleasers, it is often what keeps them in imbalanced relationships in the first place.

However, this is also true, the space you create by releasing relationships that drain you is the same space that genuinely nourishing friendships can grow into. You cannot have both at once. If your time and energy are entirely consumed by one-sided relationships, there is nothing left for the ones that could really matter.

Letting go of what drains you is not the path to loneliness. It is the path toward genuine connection.

Reflection Questions

1. Think of your closest friendships. In which friendships do you feel genuinely seen and reciprocated? In which friendships do you feel like you give more than you receive?
2. Is there a friendship you have been maintaining out of guilt or history rather than genuine connection? What would it mean to let it find its natural level?
3. When was the last time a friend asked how you were doing and really listened to the answer? How did that feel?
4. What do you fear would happen if you were honest with a friend about something that has not been working?
5. What would your friendships look like if you only maintained the ones where you felt genuinely valued?

Your Chapter 8 Practice

This week, notice how you feel after spending time with or talking to each of your close friends. Not during but after. Do you feel energized, neutral, or depleted?

You do not have to do anything with that information yet. Just gather it honestly. The data you collect this week will tell you more than any checklist about where your energy is going and whether it is being returned. Awareness is always the first step. Sometimes, just seeing clearly is enough to start making different choices.

Chapter 9: Boundaries in Romantic Relationships

People-pleasers tend to abandon themselves most completely in romantic relationships.

The stakes feel highest here because the fear of loss is strongest and the desire for connection runs deepest.

Somewhere along the way, many people absorbed the idea that love requires selflessness, that to be a good partner means making yourself smaller, more accommodating, less of a problem.

You begin to reshape yourself, adjusting your preferences, schedule, and opinions. You overlook what bothers you, keep your needs quiet so they do not feel like a burden, and give more than you receive, convincing yourself that this is what love looks like.

It is not. Love does not ask you to disappear. A relationship where you have disappeared is not the relationship either of you actually wanted.

The People-Pleaser in a Relationship

People-pleasers bring a specific pattern into romantic relationships, and it tends to show up early. In the beginning, the accommodating nature reads as easygoing, low-maintenance, and caring. Partners often love it at first.

But over time, the dynamic begins to shift. When one person consistently defers, the other, even someone with good intentions, can begin to take more without realizing it. Over time, the balance shifts.

The people-pleaser begins to feel resentful but says nothing. The partner remains unaware because nothing has been communicated. The resentment builds quietly until it surfaces indirectly through withdrawal, passive aggression, or an outburst over something small.

The people-pleaser then feels guilty for the eruption and goes back to accommodating. The cycle repeats.

This is not about blame. It is about pattern. Patterns can be changed, but only if someone names them first.

What Losing Yourself in a Relationship Looks Like

You no longer know what you want, for dinner, for the weekend, or for your life, because you have spent so much time deferring that your own preferences have faded into the background.

You monitor your partner's mood and adjust your behavior accordingly, walking on eggshells around their emotional state.

You do not bring up things that bother you because you do not want to start a conflict.

You have given up interests, friendships, or habits because they caused friction in the relationship.

You feel responsible for your partner's happiness and guilty when they are upset, even when what they are upset about has nothing to do with you.

You say yes to things you do not want because saying no feels too risky.

You find yourself becoming whoever you sense your partner needs you to be, rather than who you actually are.

If several of these feel true, you are not necessarily in a bad relationship with your partner. You are in a bad relationship with yourself, and that is what has to change first.

Limits Are the Foundation, Not the Threat

Here is the reframe that changes everything. A relationship without limits is not more intimate; it is less safe.

When you have no lines, your partner never knows where you actually stand. They cannot trust your yes because they know you say yes to everything. They cannot read your mood because you are always performing fine. They do not know the real you because you have been presenting a managed version of yourself.

Genuine intimacy requires two whole people. Not one whole person and one person-shaped accommodation. When you show up with your actual preferences, your actual limits, your actual feelings, that is when a real relationship becomes possible.

Setting a limit in a relationship is not an act of hostility; it is an act of honesty, and honesty, even when uncomfortable, is what love is built on.

Common Violations in Romantic Relationships

Emotional dismissal. Your feelings get minimized, explained away, or turned back on you. You are too sensitive. You always overreact. I was just joking. Over time, you stop sharing feelings because you have learned they will be dismissed. This compounds quietly until you stop trusting your own emotional experience.

Contempt and disrespect. Manifests as sarcasm, eye-rolling, mockery, and condescension, as well as insults and belittling. Disagreement is a normal part of relationships. Contempt is not. Research consistently shows that contempt, not conflict, is the most corrosive force in a partnership.

Control disguised as concern. Can look like monitoring who you spend time with, expecting constant check-ins, and making negative comments about your friends or family until you begin to see them less. These patterns often start gently enough that they feel like love. However, care and control are not the same thing.

Emotional manipulation. Can take many forms, including guilt-tripping when you set a limit, sulking or withdrawing when they do not get what they want, threatening to leave when you disappoint them, and using past vulnerabilities against you in arguments. These are not relationship struggles. They are manipulation tactics that require a direct response.

Assuming access without asking. Your time, your body, your money, your space, treated as available by default rather than offered by choice. A healthy partner asks. They do not assume.

Scripts for Romantic Relationship Situations

When You Need to Raise Something That Has Been Bothering You

There is something I have been wanting to bring up. When this happens, I feel a certain way. I have not said anything because I did not want to make it a big deal, but it has stayed with me, and I think it is worth talking about.

When Your Feelings Are Being Dismissed

I hear that you see it differently. My feelings are real to me, and I need them to be taken seriously even when you do not fully understand them. I am not asking you to agree. I am asking you not to tell me my feelings are wrong.

If it continues as a pattern: I have noticed that when I share something that is bothering me, I often leave the conversation feeling worse, as if my feelings were dismissed rather than heard. That is a problem for me. Can we talk about handling that differently?

When You Need to Say No to Something Physical

You are allowed to say no to anything physical at any time, including in a committed relationship, even if you have said yes before.

Not tonight.

I am not up for that right now.

I do not want to do that.

No explanation required. A partner who respects you will accept this without pressure, without sulking, and without making you feel guilty for having a preference about your own body. If they do not, that is serious information worth taking seriously.

When You Need to Reclaim Time or Space

I need some time to myself this weekend. I am going to take a day for me. I am not pulling away. I just need that space to recharge.

You do not need to justify the need for time alone. A healthy partner will understand. If time alone is consistently treated as rejection, that is worth examining.

Growing Into Yourself Inside a Relationship

If you have been a people-pleaser in your relationship, showing up differently will feel uncomfortable for both of you. Your partner has adjusted to a certain version of you. When that version starts having opinions, saying no, and taking up more space, there will be an adjustment period.

Some partners will welcome it because they have sensed the imbalance. They have been wanting more of the real you and will lean into the change.

Others will resist it. The dynamic worked for them, and your limits disrupt that. They may push back, escalate, or try to restore the old pattern through guilt or withdrawal.

How your partner responds to you as you grow into yourself is some of the most important information your relationship will ever give you. Pay attention to it.

When Control Is Showing Up as Concern

I have noticed that when I spend time with this person or make plans without checking with you first, it creates tension. I want us to have a good relationship, and I also need to be able to maintain my friendships and make my own plans without that being a problem. Can we talk about that?

Stay calm. Stay specific. And watch the response closely: whether they hear you or whether they find a way to make your limit the problem.

If the pattern continues, it is worth examining whether what is being called concern is actually control. Care and control are not the same thing. Care says I want you to be safe and happy. Control says I need to know where you are and who you are with. Care expands your world. Control slowly contracts it.

When the Relationship Itself Is the Problem

This chapter assumes a relationship where both people are fundamentally decent and capable of growth is worth working on. Some relationships are not like that.

Some partners will welcome it because they have sensed the imbalance. They have wanted more of the real you, and they will lean into the change.

If your partner consistently dismisses your feelings, controls your behavior, manipulates you emotionally, or punishes you for having needs, these are not communication problems to be solved with better scripts. They are patterns of mistreatment that scripts will not fix.

In those situations, the most important limit is what you are willing to keep accepting. You might consider couples therapy with a clear timeline for change, individual therapy to help you see the situation clearly, or a decision to leave.

You are not required to stay in a relationship that consistently makes you feel smaller. That is not love; it is endurance, and you deserve more than that.

If you are in a relationship where you feel afraid of your partner's reactions, or where there is physical intimidation or violence, you do not have to handle it alone. You can reach the National Domestic Violence Hotline at 1-800-799-7233.

Reflection Questions

1. In what ways have you made yourself smaller in your current or most recent relationship? What did you give up?
2. What topic do you avoid bringing up with your partner because you are afraid of their reaction? What does that avoidance cost you?
3. When your partner is upset, do you automatically feel responsible? Where did that pattern come from?
4. What would it look like to show up genuinely as yourself in your relationship?
5. What is one limit you have been wanting to set in your relationship but have not? What are you afraid will happen if you set it?

Your Chapter 9 Practice

This week, notice one moment where you automatically defer. Where you say whatever you want or I do not mind when you actually do have a preference.

In that moment, try something different. Say what you actually want. It does not have to be a big declaration. It can be as simple as naming a restaurant, suggesting a movie, or saying actually I would rather not.

You have been quiet about your preferences for a long time. Finding your voice again starts with the small things. Let this be one of them.

Chapter 10: Boundaries with Toxic and Narcissistic People

Every strategy in this book so far assumes that the person on the other side of your limit is a reasonable person who, once they understand how their behavior affects you, is willing and able to adjust.

That assumption breaks down completely with toxic and narcissistic people.

With a narcissist or someone with deeply toxic patterns, the standard approach, calm conversation, honest expression of feelings, and clear communication about what you need, does not just fail. It can make things worse. This is because the person you are talking to is not processing your words the way a healthy person would. They are processing them as a challenge to overcome, a weakness to exploit, or an opportunity to turn the situation back around on you.

This chapter is different from the others. It is not about how to have a better conversation. It is about how to protect yourself when better conversations are not possible.

Why Narcissistic People Are Different

Narcissistic personality disorder is a clinical diagnosis. But narcissistic behavior exists on a spectrum, and many people exhibit enough of the pattern to make ordinary limit-setting ineffective.

What characterizes narcissistic behavior, whether clinical or not, is a fundamental inability or unwillingness to treat your needs, feelings, or perspective as genuinely mattering. Not temporarily or in specific situations, but as a consistent pattern.

For the narcissist, your set limit is not a reasonable expression of your needs. It is seen as a challenge to their control over you, whether that control is real or assumed.

It becomes evidence, in their mind, that you do not love or respect them enough. It is also treated as an opportunity to prove that your limits do not actually apply to them.

This is why explaining yourself to a narcissist does not work. The problem is not that they do not understand your limit. The problem is that they do not believe your limit deserves to exist.

The Tactics They Use When You Set a Limit

Recognizing these patterns is the first line of defense.

DARVO stands for Deny, Attack, Reverse Victim and Offender. They deny that anything happened, attack your character or credibility, and position themselves as the real victim of your unreasonable behavior. You came to address their actions and somehow ended up defending your own.

The surge of guilt comes as a rush of reminders about everything they have done for you, every sacrifice they have made, and every way you have fallen short. It is meant to make your limit feel like ingratitude and to wear down your willingness to hold on to any limits set.

Gaslighting involves repeatedly denying what you experienced, telling you it did not happen, that you are imagining things, or that you are too sensitive. It is delivered with enough confidence that you begin to question your own perception of reality.

The smear campaign means that when you pull back or set a limit, they tell others their version of events first. Family members, mutual friends, anyone who might be a source of support for you gets a version of the story that makes them doubt you.

Love bombing and hoovering means after you pull back, they may suddenly become the person you always wished they were. Warm, attentive, apologetic. This is designed to pull you back in, to remind you of the good times and make you doubt that the bad times were as bad as you remember. It is called hoovering because it is designed to vacuum you back into the dynamic.

Escalation means that when a normal person encounters a limit, they adjust. When a narcissist encounters a limit, they may escalate, becoming louder, more aggressive, or more intrusive, to demonstrate that your limit is not real.

The Three Strategies That Actually Work

When involved with toxic and narcissistic people, you need a different toolkit. These strategies are not about changing the relationship. They are about protecting yourself within it the relationship, or as you leave the relationship.

The Gray Rock Method

The gray rock method is a simple concept in which you become as uninteresting and unreactive as a gray rock. You give them nothing to work with.

Narcissists are energized by your reactions, your hurt, your anger, your attempts to explain or justify yourself. When you stop providing that fuel, you become less interesting to them.

What gray rock looks like in practice: short, flat, neutral responses. Okay. I see. Thanks for letting me know. No emotional content. No explanations, no justifications, no defensiveness. No personal information. No reaction to provocations.

Gray rock script examples:

Them: You have been so distant lately. What is wrong with you?

You: I have just been busy. End of response. No elaboration.

Them: You used to be so much fun. I do not know what happened to you.

You: Mm. No defense. No explanation. No engagement with the bait.

Them: I heard you told someone something about me.

You: I am not going to get into that. Said calmly, once, and not repeated.

The Medium Chill Approach

Medium chill is a variation designed for situations where you must maintain ongoing contact such as co-parenting, family events, workplace situations. It is warmer than gray rock but equally protective.

With medium chill, you engage with surface-level topics, logistics, and neutral subjects, while keeping anything personal, emotional, or meaningful entirely off the table.

Engage with logistics, not emotions. I will have the kids back by six. Not I am feeling overwhelmed by the schedule.

Acknowledge without engaging. I hear you feel that way. Not let me explain why you are wrong.

Redirect to practical matters. Let us focus on what we need to decide today.

No Contact or Limited Contact

When someone is consistently toxic, when gray rock and medium chill are not sufficient to protect you, when the relationship is causing ongoing harm, no contact or significantly limited contact is a valid and sometimes necessary choice.

No contact means exactly what it sounds like, you stop all communication. No calls, no texts, no emails, no responding to messages sent through third parties.

Limited contact means you reduce interaction to the minimum required, perhaps only at unavoidable family events, perhaps only in writing, perhaps only regarding a specific subject like children.

These are not dramatic choices. They are not evidence that you are being unforgiving or holding a grudge. They are acknowledgments of a simple truth: some people are not safe for you to be in regular contact with, and protecting yourself from harm is a reasonable priority.

The No JADE Rule

JADE stands for Justify, Argue, Defend, Explain. With toxic and narcissistic people, doing any of these is almost always a mistake.

When you justify your limit, you imply it needs justification. When you argue, you engage on their terms. When you defend yourself, you accept that you need defending. When you explain, you invite them to find the flaw in your explanation and use it against you.

State your limit once, clearly, without elaboration. Then hold it without further discussion.

Without JADE: I am not going to be able to make it to the event.

With JADE: I cannot make it because I have a prior commitment, and I know it seems like I am always making excuses, but this was scheduled before you told me about the event, and I tried to see if I could rearrange things but could not, so I hope you understand that I am not trying to avoid you.

The first version gives them nothing to work with. The second gives them five different threads to pull.

When They Refuse to Accept Your Limit

Their acceptance of your limit is not required for your limit to be real.

They can argue. They can refuse to acknowledge it. They can tell you that you are being unreasonable. None of that changes what you will and will not accept.

A limit is not a negotiation. It is a decision you make about your own life. Their opinion of that decision is irrelevant to whether you hold it.

What changes when they push back is not your limit. What changes is the consequence.

I have told you I will not discuss this topic. If you bring it up again, I will end this call.

Then, if they bring it up again, you end the call. No warning. No additional explanation. The consequence follows the behavior, every time, without drama.

Consistency is the only language that works here. Not because it will change them. But because it changes what they can get away with.

Protecting Your Mental Health

Dealing with a narcissistic or toxic person wears down your sense of reality, your confidence, and your ability to trust yourself. Gaslighting makes you question your own perception, DARVO casts you as the villain in your own story, and smear campaigns leave you feeling isolated.

Document everything. Keep records of communications, incidents, and patterns. When you are being gaslit, clear documentation helps you stay grounded in what happened.

Find a therapist who understands narcissistic abuse. Not every therapist does, so you should look for someone with specific experience with this pattern.

Rebuild your support network. Narcissists often work to isolate their targets. Reconnecting with people who knew you before, or building new connections outside the toxic relationship, is essential.

Trust your own perception. One of the most serious effects of narcissistic abuse is that it erodes your self-trust. Rebuilding that trust is a process, but it begins with recognizing that your experience is real.

Trust Your Own Perception

One of the deepest damages of narcissistic abuse is the erosion of self-trust. Over time, having your reality consistently denied, your feelings consistently dismissed, and your perceptions consistently contradicted, you learn to doubt what you see and feel. You start asking others to confirm your reality before you trust it. You second-guess your own memory.

Rebuilding trust in your own perception begins with a clear decision to do so, but it takes time. Your experience is real. What happened, happened. What you felt, you felt. You do not need anyone else to confirm it for it to be true.

It may sound simple, but for someone whose perception has been systematically undermined, it is one of the most radical things they can do.

Document everything. As mentioned previously, keeping records of communications, incidents, and patterns. When you are gaslit, clear documentation helps you stay grounded in what actually happened. Keeping records is not dramatic or paranoid. It is a practical way to stay anchored in reality when your experience is being denied.

Give yourself time. The effects of narcissistic abuse do not disappear the moment you set a limit or leave the relationship. Healing takes time, and it does not happen overnight. There will be days when old patterns return, when you start to doubt what you know is true, and when the pull toward familiar dynamics feels strong, even though you know better.

Give yourself the same grace you would offer a close friend in this situation. You did not choose this. You were targeted because of qualities that are genuinely good in you, your empathy, your willingness to give the benefit of the doubt, and your desire to understand and help. Those qualities are not flaws. They were exploited, and that does not change what they are.

A Soft Cross-Reference

If the patterns in this chapter feel deeply familiar, if you have been in a relationship with someone who consistently operated this way, you may find it valuable to go deeper into understanding narcissistic behavior and its effects.

This chapter gives you the tools needed to set limits. My book STOP! You May Be a Narcissist or Know One, explores these patterns in detail. It provides a clear roadmap for recognizing narcissistic behavior, understanding the patterns and motivations behind it, and learning how to protect yourself and recover from its impact.

Reflection Questions

1. Is there someone in your life whose response to your limits is to escalate, guilt you, or find a way around them? How have you been explaining that behavior to yourself?

2. Have you ever felt more confused, guilty, or self-doubting after a conflict than before it? What does that pattern suggest?
3. Where in your life have you been over-explaining or over-justifying your limits?
4. What would gray rocking look like in one specific relationship or situation in your life right now?
5. Is there a relationship where limited contact or no contact would be the most honest and protective choice?

Your Chapter 10 Practice

This week, identify one interaction with a difficult person where you would normally over-explain or justify yourself. Practice the no-JADE rule instead.

State what you need to say clearly, once, then stop. Do not fill the silence with explanations or soften your words in a way that invites debate. Say it. Hold it. Let the discomfort of not explaining be part of the practice.

You have spent years believing your limits had to be earned through enough justification. They do not. They only need to be yours.

PART THREE

Communicating Boundaries

Chapter 11: The Language of Limits

Most people know what they want to say. The challenge is finding words that actually express it, words that are clear without being cruel, firm without being hostile, and honest without turning into a forty-five-minute argument.

People-pleasers face a particular challenge here. Years of watering down what they say, adding qualifiers, apologies, and built-in ways to backtrack, have made direct language feel risky. Speaking plainly can come across as aggressive, and stating a limit without layers of padding can feel rude.

It isn't. Clarity is kindness. It shows people exactly where you stand, so they don't have to guess, you don't have to repeat yourself, and neither of you wastes time on a conversation that goes nowhere because the point was buried under hesitation.

This chapter is about language, specifically the kind that works and the kind that undermines you before you even finish your sentence.

Words That Weaken Your Limits

"I'm sorry, but..." You have nothing to apologize for. Opening a limit with an apology signals that the limit itself is wrong and invites the other person to dismiss it. Replace it with a simple, direct statement.

I just wanted to say" or "I just feel like." The word *just* minimizes your message. It shrinks your statement before it even lands and signals that it may not be worth taking seriously. Remove it entirely. "I wanted to say" is stronger. "I feel" is stronger still.

Does that make sense?" or "Is that okay?" Asking for validation at the end of a limit hands the other person the power to overrule it. You have just said something important and then immediately asked whether they agree that you should have said it. Replace it with a period. State your limit and let it stand on its own.

"I do not want to be difficult, but..." You have already lost before you started. You have accepted their framing that having a limit makes you difficult, and built your entire statement around defending yourself against that. Say the thing without the preamble.

Excessive hedging. Maybe. Kind of. Sort of. I guess. These words make limits sound like suggestions. "I kind of feel like maybe I need a little more space" is not a limit. It is a wish dressed up as a question. Replace it with clear, concrete language. "I need more space." Four words. Unmistakable.

The trailing apology. "I cannot make it, I am so sorry, I really am, I feel terrible about this." The limit gets buried in the apology. All they hear is how bad you feel, which gives them an opening to push you until you change your answer. Replace it with: "I cannot make it." Warmth is fine, but apologies belong to actual wrongs, not to having a limit.

The Four Components of a Clear Limit

Not every limit needs all four of these components. But when a situation is significant enough to require a real conversation, this framework gives you everything you need.

The observation: what you have noticed.

The feeling: how it affects you.

The limit: what you need going forward.

The consequence: what will happen if the limit is not respected.

Here is how it sounds in practice:

I have noticed that our conversations often turn to criticism of my choices. It leaves me feeling defensive and unable to be myself around you. I need those topics to be off the table when we talk. If they keep coming up, I will need to cut our conversations short.

Notice what is not in that statement: an apology, a justification, a question asking whether this is acceptable, or a softener that gives them an opening to dismiss it. Direct. Complete. Said once.

A Full Range of No Responses

No is a complete sentence. But knowing that intellectually and being able to say it without your voice rising at the end are two different things.

The warm no, for people you care about:

I cannot make that work, but I hope it goes well.

I can take on that project right now. I appreciate you thinking of me.

I am going to sit this one out. Let me know how it goes.

I cannot commit to that. I hope you find someone who can help.

The neutral no, for professional situations or acquaintances:

That does not work for me.

I will not be able to do that. I am going to pass.

No, thank you.

The firm no, for repeated requests or boundary violations:

I have already said no. My answer has not changed.

I understand you are disappointed. The answer is still no.

I am not going to discuss this further.

The no that does not explain itself:

I am not available for that.

That is not going to work for me.

No.

You are not required to provide a reason. A reason is an invitation to argue. No closes the door entirely.

When They Push Back: The Broken Record

Here is the thing about saying no clearly: people often push back. Not because you said it wrong, but because they are testing whether you mean it.

The most important thing you can do when someone pushes back is not repeat your reasoning. Repeat your limit.

Can you cover my shift this weekend?

I am not able to.

But I really need you to. I have a family thing.

I understand. I am still not able to cover it.

You have done it before. Why not this time?

I am not able to this weekend.

Notice what is happening: the limit is stated, the pushback is acknowledged, and then the same limit is restated, without new reasoning, without defensiveness, without elaboration. The broken record technique works because it gives them nothing new to argue with.

Most people will stop pushing after two or three repetitions. If they do not, that is information about them. It is not a reason to give in.

Tone and Delivery

What you say matters. How you say it matters just as much.

People-pleasers often deliver limits with built-in nonverbal apologies, an upward inflection that turns a statement into a question, averted eyes, a nervous smile that undercuts the seriousness of what is being said.

These signals leak. They tell the other person that you are not sure you mean it, which gives them permission not to take it seriously.

Confident delivery means steady eye contact. A level tone that is not aggressive or apologetic. A downward inflection at the end of the sentence, a statement, not a question. Then silence. You do not need to fill the space with qualifiers.

This takes practice, especially the silence, because the urge to soften or add something to make the other person more comfortable will be strong.

Resisting it is part of the work.

Written vs. Spoken Limits

Sometimes a limit is better delivered in writing. Sometimes it needs to happen in person. Knowing the difference matters.

Consider writing when you need to be precise and do not trust yourself to stay on track in a live conversation. When the other person tends to talk over you, derail the conversation, or gaslight you about what was said. When you need a record of having said it. When the emotional stakes are high enough that you need time to compose yourself before you will be able to speak clearly.

Consider speaking when the relationship is important and the limit is significant enough to deserve a real conversation. When you want to be able to read their response and respond in real time.

When written communication with this person tends to get misread, misused, or ignored.

If you write it, keep it simple. One email, clearly stated, that does not open a thread of negotiation. If they respond with an argument, you do not have to respond to the argument. You have already said what you needed to say.

The Limit You Have Already Said

One of the most common situations people-pleasers find themselves in is having said something once, watching it get ignored, and not knowing what to do next.

If you have already said something and it was not heard, the answer is not to say it more gently, more apologetically, or with more justification. The answer is to say it again, with a consequence attached.

I have mentioned before that I need you to knock before coming into my office. It has happened again. Going forward, if you come in without knocking, I will ask you to step back out and try again. I need you to take this seriously.

The limit is restated. The pattern is named. The consequence is specific and proportional. The request to take it seriously is direct. This is not an attack. It is clear communication from someone who knows what they need and is willing to say it repeatedly.

How Limits Land Differently When Delivered With Confidence

There is a version of limit-setting that most people-pleasers do first, before they learn to do it better. It sounds like a limit, but it functions like a request for permission.

You say the words, but your voice goes up at the end, turning a statement into a question. You make eye contact, then look away.

You add a nervous laugh. You follow the limit with a question, is that okay, does that make sense. You say it once, then in the silence that follows, you add three more sentences of qualification.

The other person, consciously or not, reads all of this and know that you are uncertain. They see that you are asking them to sanction what you just said. And so they treat it as provisional, something that can be negotiated, something that might shift if they push back.

The good news is that delivery is learnable. It takes practice, and it will feel strange at first. Saying something clearly, then going quiet and letting it land can feel aggressive if you are used to softening everything. But that discomfort fades. What replaces it is being taken seriously, which is what you were after all along.

Start with low-stakes practice. A small no, delivered clearly, to someone who is not central to your life. Notice what happens. Usually nothing catastrophic. They accept it, or they push back once and then accept it. Now you have a data point: I said no clearly and survived.

Reflection Questions

1. Which weakening phrases do you use most often, I am sorry but, just, does that make sense? In what situations?
2. Think of a limit you tried to set that did not land. Looking back, what about how you said it may have undermined it?
3. What does it feel like in your body when you say no clearly and directly? Where does the discomfort live?
4. Who in your life pushes back hardest when you say no? How have you been responding to that pushback?
5. What would it feel like to say something once, clearly, and then be done with it?

Your Chapter 11 Practice

This week, pay attention to your language when you are setting a limit or saying no. Notice the qualifiers, the apologies, the trailing questions.

Pick one interaction where you would normally soften your no, and deliver it without the softeners. Warm, if the relationship calls for it, but direct. No just. No I am sorry but. No does that make sense.

Then sit with whatever comes up. The discomfort of being clear is temporary. The relief of having said what you actually meant is lasting.

Chapter 12: Having the Conversation

Knowing what to say is only half the challenge. The other half is knowing when to say it, where to say it, and what to do when the conversation does not go the way you planned.

People-pleasers tend to have limited conversations at the worst possible moments: in the middle of an argument when emotions are high, through text message when nuance gets lost, or not at all because they keep waiting for the perfect moment that never arrives.

This chapter is about the logistics of difficult conversations. Not the words themselves, but everything around them such as the setup, the timing, the environment, and the recovery when things go sideways.

Before the Conversation

Get Clear on What You Actually Need

Before you open your mouth, know what you are asking for. This sounds obvious, but it is not. People often enter a limit conversation with a vague sense of discomfort and no clear picture of what the resolution looks like.

Ask yourself: What specific behavior needs to change? What do I need to happen differently going forward? What am I willing to accept, and what am I not?

The clearer you are before the conversation, the harder it is for the other person to muddy the waters once you are in it.

Know Your Non-Negotiables

There is a difference between the limit and the conversation about it. The limit is yours. It does not change based on how they respond. But being clear about that before you start means you will not get talked out of it midway through.

Write it down in one sentence if that helps; what you need. That sentence is what you are there to communicate. Everything else, the explanation, the history, the feelings, is context. The limit is the point.

Choose Your Timing Carefully

There is no perfect moment; however, avoiding the bad ones dramatically improves your odds.

Avoid having the conversation in the middle of an argument. You are both activated, neither of you is hearing clearly, and whatever gets said will be remembered through the filter of the fight.

Avoid times when either of you is exhausted, hungry, or stressed about something unrelated. Limit conversations require bandwidth.

Avoid right before a significant event, a holiday, a trip, or a work deadline. The conversation deserves space.

Avoid public situations where either of you would feel exposed or constrained.

Avoid text or instant messaging for anything significant. Text strips tone, invites misreading, and creates a written record that can be taken out of context.

Aim for a calm moment when neither of you is in crisis mode. Choose a private space with enough time to actually talk. A time when you have had a chance to prepare what you want to say. When you are regulated, not perfectly calm, but not so flooded that you cannot think clearly.

Decide Whether to Give Them a Heads-Up

For significant conversations, especially in close relationships, giving the other person a brief head-up can help. Not a full preview, just enough so they are not blindsided:

I would like to talk about something that has been on my mind. Can we find some time this week?

This gives them a chance to show up without immediately becoming defensive from being caught off guard. It also signals that you are taking the conversation seriously, which often means they will too.

For less significant limits, or with people who would use advance notice to prepare a counterattack, you may choose to address it in the moment instead.

During the Conversation

Start With the Limit, Not the History

One of the most common mistakes in these conversations is leading with the full backstory, every incident, every time this has come up before, and every piece of evidence for why the limit is justified.

This almost always backfires. It gives the other person multiple entry points for arguing and debating specific incidents. Suddenly you are relitigating the past instead of establishing what needs to change going forward.

Start with the present. What do you need now? Say that first. The history can be context if it is needed, but it is not the headline.

Use I Statements, Not You Accusations

You always do this. You never listen. You make me feel invisible.

These statements may be true. But they open with an attack, which means the other person's first response is defense rather than listening. When someone is busy defending themselves, they are not fully listening to you.

You statement: You always dismiss my feelings when I try to talk to you.

I statement: When I bring something up, and the conversation moves on before I feel heard, I end up pulling back. That has been happening a lot lately, and I want to talk about it.

Same issue. Completely different entry point. The second version gives them something to respond to rather than a position to defend.

Say It Once, Clearly

State your limit once. Clearly. Then stop talking.

The instinct will be to keep going, to fill the silence, to add more explanation, or to soften what you just said. Resist it. The silence after a clear statement is not a problem to be solved. It is space for the other person to take in what you said.

When you keep adding to it, you dilute the original statement. You give them more threads to pull. You signal uncertainty about what you just said. Say it. Then let it land.

Listen to Their Response, Really Listen

A limit conversation is not a speech. Once you have said what you needed to say, the other person gets to respond. And how you listen to that response matters.

Listen for whether they understand what you are saying. Are they engaging with it honestly? Are they defensive but willing? Are they dismissing it entirely?

You do not have to agree with their response. You do not have to change your limit because of their response. But genuinely hearing them, rather than just waiting for your turn to talk, keeps the conversation from becoming a standoff.

Stay on Topic

Difficult conversations have a way of expanding into every unresolved issue in the relationship. The kitchen-sink phenomenon, where one issue opens the floodgates to every other grievance, can derail an otherwise productive conversation.

If they bring up something unrelated, acknowledge it and redirect:

That is worth talking about, and I want to talk about it separately. Right now I would like to stay focused on what I brought up.

You are not avoiding their concern. You are keeping this conversation functional by not letting it become about everything at once.

When It Goes Sideways

Even the best-prepared, most clearly delivered limit conversation can go sideways. Here is how to handle the most common derailments.

They Get Defensive

Defensiveness is normal. It does not mean the conversation has failed. It means they felt challenged, which is what happens when someone has been operating a certain way and you are saying it needs to change.

Do not match their defensiveness. Do not apologize for having the conversation. Do not back down from the limit to make them more comfortable.

I understand this is hard to hear. I am not trying to attack you. I am trying to tell you what I need.

Then let them sit with it. Defensiveness often settles if you do not escalate it.

They Turn It Around on You

Well, if you had not done this, I would not have done that. Or: you are one to talk. Or: what about all the times you...

This is a deflection that shifts the conversation away from their behavior and onto yours. It may be partially valid. Your behavior is worth examining. But it is not what this conversation is about.

I am willing to talk about my part in things. That is not what I brought up today. I would like to finish what I started.

You are not dismissing their concern. You are declining to be derailed by it.

They Shut Down

Some people go silent when confronted with something difficult, not as manipulation, but because they genuinely do not know how to respond in the moment. They need time to process.

If someone shuts down, do not try to force a resolution right then. Give them an out that keeps the conversation open:

It seems like you need some time to think about this. That is okay. Can we come back to it by the end of the week?

Then follow through on coming back to it. The conversation is not over just because it got paused.

They Cry

Tears derail many limit conversations because the person setting the limit suddenly feels responsible for causing pain and shifts into comfort mode, abandoning what they came to say.

Their distress is real. And it does not change what you needed to say.

You can acknowledge the emotion without abandoning the limit:

I can see this is bringing up a lot for you. I am not trying to hurt you. And I still need you to hear what I said.

Compassion and clarity are not opposites. You can hold both at once.

They Agree, and Then Nothing Changes

This is one of the most frustrating outcomes: they heard you, they agreed, they said all the right things, and two weeks later the behavior is exactly the same.

This is when the consequence becomes necessary. Without follow-through, limits are just statements.

We talked about this a few weeks ago and I want to revisit it. The situation I described has not changed. I need it to. If it does not, I am going to have to follow through on what I said.

Then follow through. Every time you state a consequence and do not enforce it, you teach the other person that your limits are not real. Every time you enforce it, you teach them that your limits are real.

After the Conversation

A limit conversation, even a successful one, takes something out of you. Give yourself time to decompress before evaluating how it went.

Ask yourself: Did I say what I needed to say? Did I hold my limit under pressure? Did I stay on topic?

You do not need a perfect conversation to have a successful one. You need one where the limit was communicated clearly and you did not abandon it. If you did those two things, the conversation served its purpose regardless of how the other person responded.

Their response is their work. Your communication is yours. You can only control one of those things.

Reflection Questions

Think of a difficult conversation you have been avoiding. What are you telling yourself is the reason you have not had it yet?

When is the worst time you have tried to set a limit or have a hard conversation? What made it hard?

What happens in your body when a conversation starts to go sideways? How do you usually respond, and is that response helping you?

Have you ever had someone agree to something and then not follow through? How did you handle it? How do you wish you had?

What would it mean to have a conversation that did not go perfectly but still accomplished what you needed it to accomplish?

Your Chapter 12 Practice

Identify one conversation you have been avoiding. It does not have to be the hardest one. Just one that needs to happen.

Write out three things before you have it: what you need to say, when and where you will say it, and what you will do if they push back or try to derail it.

You do not have to have it this week. But you do have to stop treating someday like a plan. Pick a timeframe. Write it down. That is step one.

The conversation you have been avoiding has been living in your body as low-grade dread. Deciding when it will happen takes some of that weight off because now it has a place to land.

Chapter 13: When Guilt Shows Up

The title of this book is Boundaries Without Guilt. But that title is not a promise that guilt disappears when you set a limit. It is a promise that guilt does not have to be the reason you do not.

Guilt will show up. Almost certainly. Especially in the beginning, especially with people who matter to you, especially when they are unhappy about the limit you have set. You will feel it before the conversation ends. You will feel it at three in the morning when you replay what you said. You will feel it when they go quiet, when they push back, or when they tell you that you have hurt them.

This chapter is not about getting rid of guilt. It is about understanding it well enough that you stop letting it make your decisions for you.

Two Kinds of Guilt

Not all guilt is the same. Understanding the difference is one of the most useful things you can do for yourself in this work.

Healthy guilt is your moral compass doing its job. It shows up when you have genuinely done something wrong: when you have been unkind, dishonest, or unfair. When you have acted against your own values. When you have actually harmed someone.

Healthy guilt is useful. It points to something real that needs to be addressed. When you respond to it appropriately, it resolves because you have done what it was asking you to do.

False guilt is what people pleasers know best. It is the guilt that shows up not because you have done something wrong, but because someone else is unhappy and you have been trained to feel responsible for everyone's emotional state.

False guilt arrives when you say no to a reasonable request. When you take time for yourself. When you hold a limit that someone does not like. When you stop doing something that was hurting you.

False guilt feels exactly like healthy guilt. It sits in the same place in your body. It sounds like the same internal voice. The difference is what it is responding to: not a genuine wrong, but a perceived one.

How to Tell the Difference

When guilt shows up after you have set a limit, ask yourself these questions.

Did I actually do something wrong? Not did someone get hurt or is someone unhappy. Did I act against my values? Did I lie, manipulate, or intentionally harm? If yes, that is worth examining. If no, if the only thing you did was have a limit, move to the next question.

Was the limit reasonable? Reasonable means: was it within the range of what a healthy person might need in this situation? Was it about protecting yourself, your time, your energy, or your peace?

Am I responsible for how they feel about my limit? You are responsible for your actions. You are not responsible for other people's emotional responses to those actions. They are allowed to feel disappointed. Those feelings are theirs to manage, not yours to prevent.

Would I tell a friend this was wrong? If your closest friend described your exact situation and asked whether they did something wrong, what would you say?

Where False Guilt Comes From

False guilt does not appear out of nowhere. It was installed, usually early, by people and systems that needed you to prioritize their comfort over your own needs.

Parents who responded to your no with disappointment, withdrawal, or punishment trained you to associate having limits with being bad.

Relationships where love was conditional on compliance taught you that you had to earn safety by being agreeable.

Cultural and family messages about selfishness, sacrifice, and what good people do created a framework where your needs were always secondary.

Understanding where it came from does not make it disappear overnight. But it does change the relationship you have with it. When the guilt voice says you are being selfish, you can notice it and ask: whose voice is that, really? And is it telling me the truth about this situation?

The Guilt-Obligation Loop

Here is the cycle that keeps people pleasers stuck.

You set a limit or say no. Guilt arrives. You interpret the guilt as evidence that you did something wrong. You soften the limit, apologize, or reverse course to make the guilt go away. The guilt temporarily resolves, but so does the limit. The next time a similar situation comes up, the guilt arrives faster and louder because it has been reinforced.

The guilt-obligation loop teaches you that guilt is a stop sign. That when it shows up, the right response is to give in. The only way to break the loop is to stay with the discomfort of the guilt without acting on it. To let it be there, acknowledge it, and hold your limit anyway.

Every time you hold a limit through the guilt, the guilt loses a little of its power. It still shows up. But it stops being able to control you.

The Guilt-Obligation Loop in Practice

Here is what the loop looks like in real life. You tell a family member you cannot make it to their event. The guilt arrives immediately, even before they have reacted. You apologize twice. You explain more than the situation requires. You offer to make it up to them in two other ways. And by the end of the conversation, you have not quite taken back your no, but you have made it so costly that you cannot enjoy having held it.

That is the guilt-obligation loop in action. The guilt arrived, and instead of sitting with it and letting it pass, you tried to resolve it by softening the limit until the guilt temporarily quieted.

The problem is that the next time this comes up, the guilt will arrive faster and louder because it has learned that it works. Every time you respond to false guilt by backing down, you reinforce the pattern. The guilt becomes more insistent because you have taught it that insistence produces results.

Breaking the loop means doing something different. Not refusing to feel the guilt, because you cannot control that. But refusing to act from it. Letting it be there, examining it, and choosing your behavior based on something other than its urgency.

This is uncomfortable. It is supposed to be. Growth that costs nothing is not growth. The discomfort of sitting with guilt without acting on it is the price of breaking a pattern that has been running your life for years. It is a price worth paying.

What to Do When Guilt Arrives

Name it. The moment you can name what you are feeling, this is guilt, you create a small amount of distance between yourself and the feeling. You become the observer of the guilt rather than just the person drowning in it.

Examine it. Ask the questions from earlier in this chapter. Did I do something wrong? Was my limit reasonable? Is this healthy guilt or false guilt?

Sit with it. Once you have named it and examined it, you have to be willing to sit with the discomfort without immediately resolving it by giving in. Guilt is uncomfortable. But discomfort is not the same as wrongdoing. You can feel terrible and still have done nothing wrong.

Remind yourself of the truth. When the guilt is loudest, your rational mind is quietest. Having a few true sentences ready gives you something to hold onto.

I am allowed to have limits.

Disappointing someone is not the same as harming them.

Their discomfort with my no is theirs to manage, not mine to prevent.

I can feel guilty and still be right.

Taking care of myself is not a betrayal of anyone.

Do not apologize for the limit. When you apologize, you confirm, to yourself and to the other person, that the limit was a wrongdoing. You can be warm. You can acknowledge their feelings. But apologizing for having a limit teaches your nervous system that limits require an apology, and the next one will be harder to hold.

When Guilt Is Being Used Against You

Sometimes the guilt you feel is not just an internal response to a limit. It is the result of someone actively working to make you feel guilty, using your sensitivity against you to get what they want.

Guilt-tripping sounds like:

After everything I have done for you.

I just thought you cared more about this family than that.

Fine. I will just manage alone. Do not worry about me.

I am not angry. I am just disappointed.

You have really hurt me. I hope you know that.

I guess I know where I stand.

These statements are designed to transfer responsibility for their feelings onto you, to make your limit the cause of their pain, and to use that pain as leverage to change your answer.

The response to guilt-tripping is the same as the response to any other pushback: acknowledge, do not engage, hold the limit.

I can hear that you are upset. My answer has not changed.

You do not have to defend yourself against guilt-tripping. You do not have to prove that you are a good person. You do not have to make them feel better about not getting what they wanted. You just have to not give in.

Guilt and Self-Compassion

Here is something that often gets missed: being hard on yourself for feeling guilty does not help. Telling yourself you should not feel it, that you are weak for feeling it, or that you have read all the books and should be past this, just adds another layer of suffering on top of the original.

You feel guilty because you are a person who cares about other people. That is not a character flaw. It is a feature of your humanity that got exploited by the wrong people and the wrong systems until it became a liability instead of a strength.

You are allowed to feel the guilt and be kind to yourself about feeling it. You are allowed to say: this is hard. I am doing something new and it does not feel good yet. That makes sense.

The goal is not to become someone who never feels guilty. The goal is to become someone who feels it, examines it honestly, and does not let it make decisions that belong to you.

Reflection Questions

Think of a recent time you felt guilty for having a limit or saying no. Was it healthy guilt or false guilt? What is the difference in that specific situation?

What does guilt feel like in your body? Where do you feel it? How does it usually start?

Who in your life is most effective at making you feel guilty? What do they do or say that triggers it? What do you usually do in response?

What would it mean to feel guilty and hold your limit anyway? Can you think of a time you have done that, even briefly?

What is the story you tell yourself about what kind of person you are when you disappoint someone? Where did that story come from?

Your Chapter 13 Practice

This week, when guilt shows up, write it down instead of acting on it.

Write: What happened. What limit I set or what I said no to. What the guilt is saying. Whether it is healthy guilt or false guilt. What the truth of the situation actually is.

You do not have to do anything else. You do not have to make it stop, resolve it, or convince yourself you are fine. Just document it. Put it outside your head and onto paper where you can look at it.

You will likely find that most of the guilt, written out and examined, is false. The old voice doing what it was taught to do. Seeing it clearly is the first step to not being run by it.

Chapter 14: Handling Pushback

You said it clearly. You held your tone. You did not over-explain. You set the limit and you meant it.

And then they pushed back.

Pushback is the moment most people pleasers crumble. Not because they do not mean their limit. Not because they have suddenly changed their mind. But because the discomfort of someone else's resistance is so familiar, so activating, that the urge to make it stop by giving in is almost overwhelming.

This chapter is about that moment. What pushback actually is, why it happens, what forms it takes, and exactly how to hold your ground through each of them.

What Pushback Actually Tells You

When someone pushes back against your limit, the first thing most people-pleasers feel is doubt. Maybe I was too harsh. Maybe I am being unreasonable. Maybe I should reconsider.

Here is the reframe: pushback is not evidence that your limit was wrong. Pushback is information about the other person.

A person who respects you may express disappointment. They may ask a clarifying question. They may need a moment to adjust. And then they accept the limit because they understand that your no belongs to you.

A person who pushes persistently, escalates, or refuses to accept your no is showing you that they believe your limit requires their approval to be valid. That is not true. And their belief that it does is their issue, not a reason for you to abandon what you know you need.

The intensity of someone's pushback tells you how accustomed they have become to getting their way with you. It is not a measurement of how wrong your limit is.

The Seven Forms of Pushback

The repeat ask. They simply ask again and again, with slightly different wording, as if a better-phrased request will change your answer. The repeat ask works on people pleasers because it implies your no was not quite heard correctly.

How to handle it: I heard you the first time. My answer is still no.

The why interrogation. But why? Give me one good reason. What is your reason? That is not a good enough reason. The why interrogation is designed to get you to justify your limit and then dismantle your justification. Every reason you give becomes a target.

How to handle it: I do not need to give a reason. My answer is no. You are allowed to decline without explanation. You are allowed to say because I do not want to and have that be sufficient.

The minimizer. It is not that big a deal. You are making a mountain out of a molehill. Other people do not have a problem with this. You are so sensitive. The minimizer tries to convince you that what you are protecting is not worth protecting.

How to handle it: It is a big deal to me. That is what matters. You do not need external validation that your limit is legitimate. Your experience of something determines whether you need protection from it.

The emotional escalation. They raise their voice. They cry. They get cold and distant. They become visibly upset in a way that makes you feel responsible for their emotional state. Emotional escalation hits the core wound directly: the belief that you are responsible for managing other people's feelings.

How to handle it: I can see you are upset. I am not going to change my answer while either of us is this activated. Let us come back to this when things are calmer.

Then, if necessary, leave the conversation. Leaving is not abandonment. It is a reasonable response to a conversation that has moved beyond reasonable discussion.

The bargain. Okay, what if I just. What if we compromise and. What if you did it this one time and then. The bargain feels more reasonable than other forms of pushback because it comes with apparent flexibility. But when someone has already received a clear no and immediately pivots to bargaining, they are not seeking compromise. They are seeking an opening.

How to handle it: Ask yourself: is this actually a compromise that works for me, or is it a partial version of something I have already said I do not want?

If the latter: I appreciate you looking for a middle ground, but my answer is still no on this one.

The silent treatment. They go cold. They stop responding. They become distant and monosyllabic. They make their displeasure known through absence rather than words. The silent treatment communicates: your limit has consequences for our relationship, and you should feel that consequence until you change your mind.

How to handle it: Let them have their space. Do not chase. Do not apologize. Do not start performing extra warmth to compensate for their withdrawal.

I notice things feel off between us. I am here when you are ready to talk.

Then leave it there. Their return to normal contact is their responsibility.

The consequence threat. If you do this, I am done. Fine, I will just find someone else who will. This is going to change things between us. You are going to regret this. The consequence threat is the most overt form of pushback, an attempt to raise the stakes high enough that your limit feels too costly to hold.

How to handle it: I am sorry to hear that. My answer has not changed.

If they follow through on the threat, that is information about them and the relationship. It is not evidence that you were wrong to have a limit. A relationship that requires you to abandon your needs to survive is not a relationship worth preserving at that cost.

The Internal Work During Pushback

When someone pushes back, your nervous system activates. The people-pleasing response is wired deep, which means the body treats the discomfort of someone's displeasure as a genuine threat. Your heart rate goes up. Your thinking gets cloudy. The urge to give in feels urgent and physical.

Slow your breathing deliberately. This is not a platitude. It is physiology. Slowing your breath activates the parasympathetic nervous system and literally reduces the activation that pushback triggers.

Buy yourself time if you need it. Let me think about that is not giving in. It is giving yourself space to respond from a regulated place rather than a reactive one.

Remember that their discomfort is not an emergency. It feels urgent because discomfort has always felt urgent to you. But them being unhappy with your limit is not a crisis that requires immediate resolution.

Notice the urge to give in without acting on it. You can feel the pull toward capitulation and still choose not to follow it. The urge is not a command.

When to Revisit a Limit

Not all pushback should be dismissed. There is a difference between someone pressuring you to abandon a reasonable limit and someone offering genuine information worth considering.

Revisit a limit when they have offered new information you genuinely did not have before. Not a more persuasive argument for the same position, but something that actually changes the picture. Or when you have had time to reflect and realize the limit was more reactive than considered.

Do not revisit a limit when the only thing that has changed is the intensity of their displeasure. When you are reconsidering because the guilt is loud, not because your thinking has changed. When they have worn you down through persistence rather than persuaded you through reasoning.

The distinction matters. Changing your mind because you have genuinely learned something is growth. Changing your mind because someone pushed hard enough is erosion.

After You Have Held It

When you hold a limit through pushback, when you say no, they push, and you hold, something important happens. It may not feel like a victory in the moment. You might still feel shaky, guilty, or uncertain. But you have done something your nervous system is not accustomed to.

You have broken a pattern. You have taught yourself, and them, that your limits are real. You have demonstrated to the part of you that always believed it was not safe to have needs that it survived.

Give yourself credit for that. Not performatively, not in a way that requires someone else to witness, just privately, in the quiet after the conversation. You held it. That matters.

And the next time will be a little easier. Not easy. A little easier. Because the evidence is accumulating that you can do this.

Reflection Questions

Which form of pushback is hardest for you to hold against? The emotional escalation? The silent treatment? The consequence threat? Why that one?

Think of a time you gave in to pushback on a limit you believed in. What happened after? How did you feel about yourself?

What does your body do when someone pushes back on you? Where do you feel it? What is your automatic response?

Is there someone in your life who consistently pushes back on your limits? What pattern have they learned about what works with you?

What would it mean to hold a limit through the most intense pushback you can imagine from the most significant person in your life?

Your Chapter 14 Practice

This week, when someone pushes back on a limit, notice the urge to give in without acting on it.

You can feel the pull toward capitulation and still choose not to follow it. Sit with the discomfort of their displeasure for one full minute before deciding anything. You will likely find that nothing collapses in that minute. They remain unhappy. You remain intact. And you have one more piece of evidence that their displeasure is survivable.

Chapter 15: Consequences That Mean Something

A limit without a consequence is a suggestion.

You can say it clearly. You can say it calmly. You can say it with perfect language, ideal timing, and exactly the right tone. But if nothing changes when the limit is crossed, if life goes on exactly as before, if the person who ignored your limit faces no shift in what they have access to, then what you communicated was not a limit. It was a preference. And preferences, in the minds of people who are accustomed to getting their way, are optional.

This chapter is about consequences: what they are, how to identify the right ones, how to communicate them clearly, and most importantly, how to follow through on them even when it is hard.

Because the follow-through is everything. Without it, limits are just words.

What a Consequence Actually Is

A consequence is not a punishment. You are not trying to hurt someone for crossing your limit or make them suffer for what they did.

A consequence is not a threat. A threat is designed to coerce, to scare someone into compliance through fear. A consequence is different. It is simply a description of what will happen next based on what has already happened.

A consequence is not manipulation. You are not dangling something to get what you want. You are telling the truth about what your limit means in practice.

A consequence is the natural, logical result of a limit being crossed. It answers the question: if this limit is not respected, what changes?

The answer to that question is always about what you will do, never about what you will make them do. You cannot control their behavior. You can only control your response to it.

Why Consequences Are So Hard to Follow Through On

Most people-pleasers are very good at stating consequences and very bad at following through on them. Which means they have spent years teaching the people in their lives that consequences are bluffs.

If you do that again, I am leaving. They do it again. You stay.

If this keeps happening, I am going to stop helping with that. It keeps happening. You keep helping.

I am serious this time. If you speak to me that way again, I am ending this call. They do it again. You stay on the line, backpedal, and apologize for threatening to hang up.

Every time you state a consequence and do not follow through, you do two things. You teach the other person that your limits have no real teeth. And you teach yourself that you are not actually someone who follows through, which makes the next consequence even harder to hold.

The reasons are understandable. Following through on a consequence is often painful. It means accepting the discomfort of conflict escalating, a relationship changing, or a person being hurt or angry. For someone who has spent their life avoiding exactly that discomfort, it can feel impossible.

But the pain of not following through compounds. Every time you back down, the pattern gets stronger. The other person gets bolder. And you get smaller.

How to Choose the Right Consequence

Not every limit needs a consequence attached. For minor situations or reasonable people, a clear limit stated once is often enough. Consequences become necessary when a limit has been stated and crossed, when someone has demonstrated that the limit alone is not sufficient.

A good consequence has four qualities.

It is proportional. The consequence should match the severity of the violation. A minor, repeated irritation warrants a smaller consequence, like stepping back from a conversation or reducing contact for a period. A serious violation may warrant a much more significant one.

Disproportionate consequences lose credibility. If someone borrows something without asking and your response is to end the friendship, the consequence will read as extreme. If someone has been emotionally abusive for years and your consequence is to stop answering their calls for a week, the consequence may not be sufficient.

It is within your control. The only consequences you can reliably deliver are ones that depend entirely on your own actions. If you do that again, you will lose everyone's respect is not a consequence. It is a prediction about other people's behavior that you cannot control. If you do that again, I am going to leave this conversation is a consequence because leaving is something only you have to do.

Stay in your own lane. What will you do? That is the consequence.

It is something you will actually do. This is the most important quality. A consequence you will not follow through on is worse than no consequence at all because it trains people that your limits are empty.

Before you state a consequence, ask yourself honestly: am I willing to do this? If the answer is no, do not state it. Either find a consequence you are willing to enforce or wait until you are. A consequence that you will actually follow through on is infinitely more powerful than a dramatic one you will not.

It is stated calmly, not in the heat of the moment. Consequences stated in anger often say more than you mean. They escalate to the dramatic end of the spectrum before you have thought through whether you are willing to go there. Whenever possible, state consequences when you are regulated. They land differently, and they are more likely to be the ones you will actually follow through on.

The Structure of a Consequence Statement

A consequence statement has two parts: the limit and the consequence. Together they sound like this:

When this behavior happens, I am going to take this specific action.

Simple. Direct. No threat, no drama, no extensive justification.

Examples:

When you bring up my weight in our conversations, I am going to end the call.

If you show up without calling first again, I am not going to answer the door.

If this workload continues without any change in compensation or title, I am going to start looking for other opportunities.

If you speak to me that way again in front of the kids, I am going to take them and leave for the rest of the day.

If the payment is not received by Friday, I am going to stop work on this project until it is.

Notice what each of these has in common: a specific trigger and a specific action. Not, I am going to be very upset. Not, things are going to change. A concrete, actionable thing that you will do.

Following Through: The Hardest Part

The consequence has been stated. The behavior has happened again. Now comes the moment most people pleasers have been dreading since they opened their mouth.

You have to do the thing you said you would do.

Here is what that moment feels like: the guilt arrives immediately. The voice that says maybe they did not mean it this time, maybe you are being too harsh, maybe this will break everything. The urge to let it slide just this once, which is exactly what you have been doing for years and exactly why you are here.

Here is what following through requires: acting before the guilt has time to talk you out of it.

Not impulsively. Not aggressively. Calmly and immediately.

You said you would end the call if they brought it up again. They brought it up. You say: this is the situation I mentioned. I am going to end the call now. We can talk another time.

And then you end the call.

You do not explain further. You do not apologize. You do not wait to see if they will push back and then reconsider. You do the thing you said you would do. That is it. That is the whole move.

What Happens After You Follow Through

The first few times you follow through on a consequence, the other person will likely escalate. They have learned that pressure works with you, that if they push hard enough, long enough, you will give in. When the expected capitulation does not come, they may push harder.

This is sometimes called an extinction burst. The behavior gets worse before it gets better because the person is doing more of what has always worked, confused about why it is not working now.

It will pass. If you hold the consequence consistently, every time the limit is crossed, the consequence follows, the pattern eventually shifts. Either they adjust their behavior or they reveal that they are unwilling to, which is also important information.

What you are building, one followed-through consequence at a time, is credibility. Credibility with the other person that your limits are real. And credibility with yourself that you are someone who means what they say.

That second kind of credibility is the more important one.

Graduated Consequences

Not every situation calls for the most serious consequence available. A graduated approach, starting with smaller consequences and escalating if needed, is often more proportional and more sustainable.

Example of a graduated consequence sequence:

First crossing: name it and restate the limit. That is the topic I mentioned. I am not going to engage with it.

Second crossing: apply a smaller consequence. I am going to step away from this conversation now. We can reconnect when this topic is off the table.

Third crossing: apply a more significant consequence. I have stepped away from this conversation twice when this came up. If it continues, I am going to need to see you less frequently.

Ongoing pattern: apply the most significant consequence available to you, which may include significantly reducing or ending contact.

Graduated consequences give the other person, and you, the chance to adjust before you reach the most significant outcome. They also demonstrate that you are not operating from anger or extremism, but from a consistent, proportional response to a repeated pattern.

Consequences and Relationships You Value

The hardest consequences to follow through on are the ones in the relationships that matter most. Because the consequence that makes sense in those relationships, pulling back, reducing contact, or changing the dynamic, also involves real loss.

Here is the truth about that: if the relationship requires you to have no limits, it is already costing you more than the consequence would. The pain of the consequence is visible and immediate. The cost of having no limits is chronic, low-grade, and invisible until it is not.

Following through on a consequence in a relationship you value is not destroying the relationship. It is finding out whether the relationship can exist on terms that are honest. If the other person adjusts, if they take your limit seriously because they see you mean it, the relationship can become stronger. If they do not, you have learned something true about what the relationship actually is.

Either outcome gives you more than the alternative, which is spending the rest of the relationship managing around a limit no one respects.

Reflection Questions

Think of a consequence you stated but did not follow through on. What stopped you? What did that teach the other person?

Is there a limit in your life right now that has been crossed repeatedly without consequence? What consequence would be proportional, within your control, and something you would actually follow through on?

What is the consequence you are most afraid to follow through on? What are you afraid will happen?

Have you ever followed through on a consequence? What happened? How did it feel afterward?

What would change in your life if the people around you believed, from experience, that you mean what you say?

Your Chapter 15 Practice

Identify one limit in your life that has been crossed at least twice without consequence. Write out a consequence statement for it: when this behavior happens, I am going to take this specific action.

Make sure it passes the four tests: proportional, within your control, something you will actually do, and stated calmly.

You do not have to deliver it today. But write it. Make it specific. Make it real. Because having the language ready is the difference between following through in the moment and finding yourself, once again, letting it slide.

Your limits are only as real as your willingness to back them up. This week, decide what backing them up actually looks like.

PART FOUR

Holding Your Ground

Chapter 16: When People Change, and When They Do Not

When you begin setting limits consistently, when you say what you mean and follow through on it, one of three things will happen with the people in your life.

Some will adjust. They will take your limit seriously, recalibrate how they treat you, and the relationship will find a new and often better equilibrium. These are people who care about you more than they care about getting their way and who are capable of growth when the situation asks for it.

Some will resist initially but eventually adapt. They push back, they test the limit, they make the adjustment difficult. And then, when they discover that the limit is real and consistent, they adapt. The relationship goes through an uncomfortable period and comes out the other side stronger.

And others will not change. No matter how clearly you communicate, no matter how consistently you hold the limit, they continue to cross it, dismiss it, or work around it. They have decided that the version of you that had no limits was the real you, and that this version, the one who holds ground, is a problem to be solved rather than a person to be respected.

This chapter is about how to recognize which is which, how to respond to each, and what to do with the grief that comes when someone you hoped would change reveals that they will not.

Real Change vs. Performed Change

It is important to distinguish between someone who is genuinely adjusting to your limits and someone who is performing adjustment while waiting for an opportunity to return to the old pattern.

Genuine change tends to look like this. The behavior actually shifts, not just their words, but what they do. They stop doing the thing you asked them to stop. They start doing the thing you asked them to do. The change shows up in action, not just in apology.

The change is consistent over time. Not perfect. People make mistakes and old habits resurface. But the general direction is toward the limit, not away from it.

They do not hold the change against you. They do not bring it up as evidence of their sacrifice or use it as leverage in other conversations. I have been trying so hard to give you what you need as a precursor to asking you to give up something is not genuine change. That is a transaction.

They take responsibility for their part without making it your job to manage their feelings about having to change. Genuine adjustment might come with discomfort for them. That discomfort is theirs to process, not yours to relieve.

Performed change has its own patterns, worth knowing because they can feel convincing in the moment.

The apology is elaborate but the behavior does not shift. They say all the right things. They may cry, they may promise, they may seem genuinely moved. And then, two weeks later, the behavior is the same.

They change for a while and then slide back. A period of compliance followed by a gradual return to the original pattern, as if testing whether enough time has passed for you to let it go.

They change the form but not the substance. If you said do not criticize my parenting, they stop doing it directly and start doing it indirectly, through sighs, implications, or comments to other people. The behavior has technically shifted but the impact has not.

They make the change contingent on your behavior. I will stop if you stop being so sensitive. The change becomes conditional, a negotiation where you are being asked to pay for it.

How Long to Give It

This is one of the most common questions: how long do you wait to see if someone will genuinely change before you accept that they will not?

There is no universal answer. But there are useful frameworks.

Consider the pattern, not the incident. One violation after a limit has been set is not the same as a pattern of violations. People make mistakes. A single recurrence, handled with a reminder and a consequence, is not proof that nothing will ever change. A recurring pattern, the same behavior across multiple clear conversations over a meaningful period of time, is different.

Consider whether anything is actually changing, not just being promised. Promises are not evidence of change. Repeated promises with no behavioral follow-through are evidence of a pattern. You are looking for change in what happens, not in what is said.

Consider what the change would require of them. Some changes are genuinely difficult. A lifetime of a certain behavior does not reverse easily, even with genuine motivation. Be realistic about what you are asking for and whether they are genuinely pursuing it.

When Someone Does Not Change

There comes a point, sometimes slowly, sometimes suddenly, when the evidence is clear. The behavior is not changing. Not because they cannot. Because they will not. Because the relationship as it has always been works for them, and your limits are an inconvenience they have decided not to accommodate.

That moment is one of the most painful in this work. Because it means accepting something you may have spent a long time hoping would not be true: that this person, in this relationship, is not going to give you what you need.

Accepting that someone will not change requires honesty with yourself first. You have to be willing to see the pattern clearly without explaining it away or finding new reasons to believe this time will be different.

It requires grief. Accepting that someone will not change is a loss. Not just of the behavior you wanted them to stop, but of the relationship you hoped it could become. That grief is real and it deserves space.

It does not require anger. You do not have to be angry at someone for being who they are. Clarity about who someone is, including clarity that who they are is not compatible with what you need, does not require bitterness to be valid.

It does not require a confrontation. You do not have to convince them that they have failed or get them to admit what they have done. Your clarity about the situation does not depend on their agreement with it.

The Decision That Follows

When someone consistently refuses to respect your limits, you face a decision. Not a comfortable one, but a clear one: what level of access to your life will this person have, given who they have demonstrated themselves to be?

The options exist on a spectrum.

Full relationship with adjusted expectations. You stay in the relationship but stop expecting it to be something it is not. You protect yourself within it and get your genuine needs met elsewhere.

Reduced contact. You scale back how often you see or speak to them, how much you share, and how much emotional energy you invest. The relationship continues but at a lower intensity.

Significant distance. Contact only at unavoidable occasions, family events, or necessary logistics, with minimal personal engagement.

No contact. You end the relationship entirely. You stop communicating, stop responding, and stop attending events where they will be present.

There is no right answer on this spectrum that applies to everyone. The right answer is the one that is honest about what the relationship is, protective of your wellbeing, and something you can actually sustain.

Grieving the Relationship You Wanted

One of the underacknowledged parts of this work is the grief that comes with accepting that someone you love is not capable of or willing to be who you needed them to be.

This grief can show up in unexpected ways. Anger that seems disproportionate to small incidents. Sadness that surfaces at odd moments. A kind of mourning that does not quite make sense because the person is still alive, still technically in your life.

What you are mourning is not the person themselves, but the version of the relationship you hoped for. The one where they showed up the way you needed them to. The one where the love was mutual and the respect was real.

That grief is legitimate. It is not weakness or self-pity. It is what happens when you love someone enough to have wanted more from the relationship than it was ever going to give.

Let yourself grieve it. Not indefinitely, not as a reason to stay stuck, but as the honest acknowledgment that something real has been lost.

What Genuine Change Asks of You

When someone does genuinely change in response to your limits, when they take you seriously, adjust their behavior, and show up differently, that asks something of you too.

It asks you to acknowledge it. Not to perform gratitude or make a big production of it, but to notice it and let it register. People who are trying deserve to know their effort is visible.

It asks you not to hold the past forever. Trust is rebuilt over time through consistent behavior. But there is a difference between appropriate caution and refusing to let someone out of the box you have put them in. If someone is genuinely changing, they deserve to experience that the relationship can actually shift.

And it asks you to stay honest. If you notice old patterns creeping back, say so early, before resentment builds, before you are back where you started. The maintenance of a changed relationship requires ongoing communication, not a one-time conversation followed by silence.

A Word on Patience With the Process

Genuine change in another person is rarely clean or linear. It tends to happen in a halting, imperfect way: improvement followed by a slide, a period of doing well followed by a single incident of the old behavior, growth that is visible in some contexts and absent in others.

If you have set a limit and someone is genuinely trying to respect it, you will likely see a pattern of mostly better with occasional lapses rather than perfect behavior. The question worth asking is not did they ever slip, but is the overall direction moving toward what you need?

A single slip after weeks of genuine effort is different from a single week of effort followed by a return to the old pattern. The difference is in the trajectory. One is growth with the inevitable messiness that growth involves. The other is performance, designed to relieve the pressure long enough for things to return to normal.

Pay attention to trajectory. And pay attention to how they respond when they slip. Does the person who is genuinely changing acknowledge the slip, take responsibility for it, and make a visible effort to correct course? Or do they minimize it, deny it, or find a way to make it your fault for noticing? That response tells you more about whether the change is real than the slip itself does.

Reflection Questions

Think of someone in your life who has changed in response to your limits. What did that change look like? How did you respond to it?

Think of someone who has not changed despite clear limits. What have you been telling yourself to explain or justify staying in the same pattern with them?

What does the grief look like for you when you accept that someone will not be who you needed them to be? Do you let yourself feel it or do you find ways to skip past it?

Where on the spectrum, full relationship, reduced contact, significant distance, no contact, does one key relationship in your life actually need to be, based on who the person has demonstrated themselves to be?

What would it mean to stop waiting for someone to change and start responding to who they actually are?

Your Chapter 16 Practice

This week, think about one relationship in your life where you have been waiting for change. Not hoping. Waiting. As in, you have already set the limit, you have already had the conversation, and you have been watching to see what happens.

Write down what you have actually observed. Not what was promised. Not what you hope is happening. What has actually changed, in behavior, consistently, over time?

Let the evidence speak. Not to make a decision today necessarily, but to see clearly what is there, and to stop confusing hope with data. Clarity, even when it is painful, is always more useful than the fog of hoping things are different than they are.

Chapter 17: Self-Respect as a Practice

Every chapter in this book is about what to do. What to say. How to hold it. What to do when they push back. How to follow through.

This chapter is about who you need to become before any of it can be sustainable.

Because here is the truth that sits underneath all the scripts and strategies: limits are not primarily a communication skill. They are an expression of self-respect. And if the self-respect is not there, if you do not genuinely believe, somewhere in your body, that you matter and that your needs are legitimate, the scripts will feel hollow and the limits will keep collapsing under pressure.

Self-respect is the foundation. Everything else is built on top of it. And unlike a script, self-respect is not something you can look up and apply in the moment. It is something you build slowly through a series of small daily choices that accumulate into a different relationship with yourself.

What Self-Respect Actually Is

Self-respect is not self-esteem in the conventional sense, the feeling of being good, capable, or worthy that fluctuates with your performance and other people's opinions. Self-esteem goes up when things go well and down when they do not.

Self-respect is steadier than that. It is the baseline conviction that you deserve to be treated with dignity, not because you have earned it through achievement or because someone has granted it to you, but because you are a human being and that is the minimum standard.

Self-respect does not require you to think you are exceptional. It does not require confidence in your abilities or certainty about your worth. It simply requires the belief, however fragile, however contested by the old voices, that your needs count. That your experience of a situation matters. That you are allowed to protect yourself.

How Self-Respect Gets Eroded

Understanding how self-respect gets lost helps explain why rebuilding it requires deliberate effort rather than just deciding to feel differently.

Every time you said yes when you meant no, you sent yourself the message that your actual answer did not matter.

Every time you apologized for having a need, you confirmed the belief that needs are problems.

Every time you absorbed someone's cruelty without naming it, you taught your nervous system that this is what you can expect.

Every time you made yourself smaller to keep the peace, you practiced the skill of disappearing.

Every time someone violated your limits without consequence, the message reinforced itself: you do not matter enough to protect.

None of this was your fault. It was the result of circumstances, relationships, and environments that taught you it was not safe to have needs. The patterns made sense at the time. They were adaptive. But you are not in those contexts anymore, or you are working to change them. And the patterns that protected you then are now the patterns that limit you.

The Daily Practices That Build Self-Respect

Self-respect is not rebuilt through a single insight or a transformative moment. It is rebuilt through repetition: the accumulated evidence of small choices, made consistently, that show you a different relationship with yourself is possible.

Keep the promises you make to yourself. This is the most direct path to self-respect. Every time you tell yourself you are going to do something, set a limit, have a conversation, or take time for yourself, and then you do it, you strengthen the internal message: I am someone who follows through for myself.

Start small. Promises you can keep. Not dramatic declarations of change, but specific, achievable commitments. I will not answer work messages after eight tonight. I will leave that conversation if it becomes disrespectful. I will take Saturday morning for myself. Then do it. The accumulation of kept small promises becomes the foundation of trust in yourself.

Honor your own experience. People pleasers have often spent so long managing other people's experiences that they have lost touch with their own. You have become fluent in other people's feelings and needs and gone quiet on your own.

Rebuilding self-respect requires getting back in touch with your actual experience. What do you feel in this situation? What do you need right now? What is your body telling you about this interaction? Practice asking yourself these questions regularly. You are a person having an experience. That experience is worth noticing.

Stop apologizing for existing. Notice how often you apologize for things that are not wrongs. For taking up time. For having a preference. For asking a question. For needing something.

Sorry, can I ask you something? Sorry, I just need a minute. Sorry, I think I might disagree with that.

These apologies seem small. They add up. Every unnecessary apology is a small statement that your presence requires justification. Start catching them. When you notice one, ask yourself, did I actually do something wrong here? If not, the apology belongs somewhere else.

Spend time doing things you value. Self-respect has a practical dimension that is not talked about enough; it requires that your life actually contain things that matter to you. Not just obligations, not just service to other people's needs, but things you do because they nourish you.

People-pleasers often have very thin lives in this sense. Full of activity. Full of responsibility. But lacking things that are done purely for themselves.

What do you enjoy? What genuinely restores you? When did you last do it?

Rebuilding your own life, with your own interests and your own sources of meaning, is not selfish. It is the precondition for having a self that can set limits from a place of genuine grounding rather than chronic depletion.

Treat yourself the way you treat people you respect. Think of someone you genuinely respect, a friend, a mentor, someone whose well-being you take seriously. Now ask: would you speak to them the way you speak to yourself? Would you tolerate someone else treating them the way you allow yourself to be treated?

The gap between how you treat people you respect and how you treat yourself is a direct measurement of your current self-respect deficit. Closing that gap, speaking to yourself with the same basic consideration you extend to others, refusing on your own behalf what you would refuse on theirs, is the work.

Self-Respect and Limits

Here is how self-respect and limits connect: limits set by self-respect feel different from those set by rules.

When you set a limit from a rule, it sounds like this: I am supposed to have limits. I read in a book that I should say no. I know I am allowed to do this. But that kind of limit is fragile. It depends on remembering the rule, believing it applies to you, and being able to hold onto it under pressure. When someone pushes back, the rule starts to wobble.

When you set a limit from self-respect, from a genuine embodied sense that this matters, that you matter, that what is being crossed is real, it is sturdier. Not unshakeable, not immune to guilt or pressure, but anchored in something deeper than a strategy. It is anchored in a relationship with yourself.

This is why the work of building self-respect is not separate from the work of setting limits. It is the work. The scripts and the strategies are tools. Self-respect is the hand that holds them.

When Self-Respect Feels Far Away

Not every day will feel like progress. There will be days when the old voices are loud, when you give in to something you meant to hold, when the guilt overwhelms you, and when you find yourself performing, accommodating, and shrinking in exactly the ways you have been trying to change.

Those days are not evidence that you are failing. They are evidence that you are human, that the patterns are old and stubborn, and that change is not linear.

On those days, the practice is not to berate yourself for falling back. The practice is to notice it without judgment and return. Not to the beginning. You are not starting over every time you slip. You are returning to a path you are still on.

Self-compassion and self-respect are not opposites. Self-compassion, the ability to treat yourself with kindness when you fall short, is actually a prerequisite for sustained self-respect. Because you cannot build a healthy relationship with yourself by being cruel to yourself when you make mistakes.

Be kind to yourself in the setbacks. Be honest with yourself about the patterns. And keep going.

Self-Respect and Relationships

Here is something that often surprises people when they begin this work: when you start treating yourself with more consistent respect, your relationships change, even before you have had a single direct conversation about limits.

People pick up on what you project about how you expect to be treated. The person who consistently accepts dismissal, who repeatedly absorbs unkindness without response, who never holds a consequence, is communicating something to everyone around them, whether they intend to or not. That communication is: this is what I accept. This is what I believe I deserve.

When you begin treating yourself differently, that communication shifts. Not dramatically, not overnight, but perceptibly. The people around you begin to adjust to what they sense from you.

That adjustment varies from person to person. For some, particularly those who care about you and were never trying to take advantage of you, it is a relief. They sensed something was off in the old dynamic, and the new version of you feels more honest, more stable, and more genuinely present.

For others, particularly those whose behavior relied on your self-neglect, the adjustment is resistance. They will push back against the change, try to restore the old pattern, or escalate to demonstrate that your new limits will not hold. That resistance is information. It tells you clearly who was there for you and who was there for what you provided.

You do not have to decide anything about these relationships immediately. Just pay attention. The responses you get when you begin to treat yourself with more respect will teach you more about your relationships than years of careful observation could.

Reflection Questions

On a scale of one to ten, how much do you genuinely believe, in your body and not just intellectually, that your needs matter as much as other people's? What would a higher number look like in practice?

What is one small promise you could make to yourself this week and keep? Something specific enough that you will know whether you did it.

When you compare how you treat people you respect to how you treat yourself, where is the biggest gap? What would it look like to close it even slightly?

What did you used to do, before people-pleasing took over, that you have stopped doing because it did not fit with always being available for others? Is there one thing you could reclaim?

What does self-respect feel like in your body on the rare occasions when you experience it? Where do you feel it? What is happening when it is present?

Your Chapter 17 Practice

This week, choose one of the daily practices from this chapter and commit to it for seven days. Not all of them. One.

Pick the one that feels most foreign. The one that makes a small part of you think: I do not really deserve to do that. That resistance is the signal. That is where the work is.

Seven days. One practice. Notice what shifts, not just in how you feel, but in how you show up in the situations where limits matter.

Self-respect is built in the quiet moments, long before the difficult conversations arrive. What you practice today is what you will have available when you need it most.

Chapter 18: Staying Consistent

Setting a limit once is hard. Maintaining it over weeks, months, and years, through the seasons of a relationship, through your own doubts, through the other person's repeated testing, is a different challenge entirely.

Most people who struggle with limits do not fail in the first conversation. They fail in the third month, when the limit has been mostly respected but they have let a few small things slide. They fail when life gets stressful and the energy required to hold their ground feels like too much. They fail when they convince themselves that things have changed enough that the old patterns will not come back.

Consistency is what transforms a limit from a single act of courage into a new way of living. This chapter is about how to build and maintain that consistency over the long haul.

Why Consistency Is So Hard

Limits erode for predictable reasons. Understanding them in advance means you can watch for them rather than being blindsided.

Compassion fatigue with your own limits. In the beginning, holding a limit feels important and urgent. You can feel why it matters. But as time passes and the immediate crisis recedes, the limit can start to feel like an overreaction. You remember the good times. The limit that once felt necessary starts to feel harsh.

This is not a sign that the limit was wrong. It is a sign that you are human and that memory softens pain. The question to ask yourself is not does this limit still feel as urgent as it did but does the reason I set it still exist?

Gradual normalization. When someone respects a limit consistently over time, it can start to feel safe enough to let small exceptions slide. But small exceptions have a way of accumulating. The limit that was once clear becomes fuzzy. The fuzzy limit becomes ignored. And one day you realize you are back where you started. Watch for the creep.

Relational pressure over time. A limit stated once faces one moment of pressure. A limit maintained over time faces the accumulated pressure of every interaction, every occasion, every conversation in which the other person tests whether it is still real. That sustained pressure wears people down in ways a single confrontation does not.

Life circumstances. Stress, loss, illness, major transitions all reduce the bandwidth available for holding limits. When you are in survival mode, the energy required to maintain healthy patterns is often the first thing to go. Limits slip. Old dynamics resurface. This is not failure. It is human. The question is not how to prevent it entirely but how to notice it and course-correct.

The Practices That Support Long-Term Consistency

Regular check-ins with yourself. Consistency requires awareness. Not obsessive monitoring, but a periodic honest look at how things are actually going. A simple monthly question: are the limits I set still being respected? Am I still holding the ones I set? Has anything drifted that needs to be addressed?

Keeping records of your own progress. People pleasers tend to have short memories for their own growth. They remember the slips vividly and forget the holds. Writing down the moments when you held a limit, when it was hard, when someone pushed back and you held anyway, creates a record of evidence you can return to when the doubt gets loud. You are building something. Document the building.

Knowing your high-risk situations. Consistency is easier when you know in advance where you are most likely to falter. High-risk situations are the ones where you historically give in: specific people, specific dynamics, specific emotional states.

For some people it is the holidays, when family pressure spikes and old dynamics reassert themselves. For others it is when they are exhausted or ill and do not have the energy to hold ground. Know your high-risk situations. Not to avoid them, you often cannot, but to go into them prepared. To have your language ready. To have thought through in advance what you are going to do if the limit gets tested.

Building a support system. Consistency is significantly easier when you have people in your life who know what you are working on and can offer a reality check when your own perspective gets cloudy. This might be a therapist, a close friend who understands the dynamic you are navigating, or a community of people doing similar work. What it needs to be is someone who will tell you the truth, not just validate whatever you are feeling in the moment.

Reaffirming why the limit exists. When a limit starts to feel like an obstacle rather than a protection, go back to why you set it. Not the incident that triggered it, but the deeper reason: what it was protecting, what it was making space for, what life looked like before it was there.

Sometimes the most powerful consistency tool is simply remembering. Remembering what the relationship felt like when there were no limits. Remembering what you felt like. That memory is not a reason to stay angry. It is a reason to stay honest.

When You Have Slipped

You will slip. At some point, under some combination of circumstances, you will give in to something you meant to hold. You will find yourself, three months into maintaining a limit beautifully, back in the old pattern.

Here is what to do when that happens.

Notice it without catastrophizing. A slip is not a collapse. It is not proof that you will never change, that all the work was for nothing, that you are fundamentally incapable of this. It is a moment of going back to the old pattern, which, given how deeply those patterns are wired, is completely understandable.

Understand what happened. What was the situation? What was your state, were you tired, stressed, depleted? What was the specific trigger? Understanding the conditions of the slip helps you prepare for the next time those conditions arise.

Correct course without drama. You do not need to have a big conversation about the fact that you slipped. You do not need to announce that you are getting back on track. You just need to return to the limit on the next opportunity. Quietly. Without making the slip itself the story.

Do not use the slip to justify more slipping. The most dangerous moment after a slip is the voice that says: well, you have already broken it, so it does not matter now. That is the voice of the old pattern looking for a door. Close it.

The Long Game

Here is what sustained consistency eventually produces, if you stay with it long enough.

People around you learn, through accumulated experience, that your limits are real. The testing reduces. Not always, not with everyone, but with most people in most relationships, consistent follow-through eventually results in a different dynamic.

You stop dreading certain interactions. The situations that used to fill you with anxiety become less threatening because you know what you will do. You have a plan. You have done it before.

Your relationship with yourself changes. The accumulation of kept promises, held limits, and followed-through consequences builds something real: trust in yourself. The sense that you are someone who means what they say. For many people pleasers, that is the thing they have been missing their entire adult lives.

Your relationships become more honest. When people know you will say what you mean, they can trust your yes. They know your kindness is not just compliance. Your presence is genuine because you are actually there, showing up as yourself.

None of this happens overnight. It is the work of months and years, not days and weeks. But it compounds. Each chapter you add to the story of who you are becoming makes the next one easier to write.

Adjusting Limits Over Time

Consistency does not mean rigidity. Limits can and do evolve as circumstances, relationships, and your own understanding of what you need change.

A limit set in a moment of acute distress may not be the right limit for the long term. A relationship that has genuinely changed may warrant different limits than it required when the damage was being done. You may discover, through experience, that what you thought you needed was slightly different from what actually works.

Adjusting a limit from a place of genuine reflection is healthy. It's different from abandoning a limit because of pressure, guilt, or the hope that things have changed when the evidence does not support it.

The question to ask when you are considering adjusting a limit is this: am I changing this because my honest assessment of the situation has changed, or am I changing it because holding it has become uncomfortable?

If it is the former, adjust. If it is the latter, hold.

Reflection Questions

1. Where have your limits drifted in the past, either gradually through normalization or suddenly under pressure? What were the conditions that allowed it?
2. What are your personal high-risk situations for limit erosion? Who are the people, what are the circumstances, what is the emotional state that makes you most likely to give in?
3. Do you have someone in your life who can offer an honest outside perspective on your limits and patterns? If not, what would it take to build that support?
4. What does a slip feel like for you internally? Do you tend to catastrophize it, minimize it, or use it as a reason to give up on the limit entirely?
5. What would your life look like two years from now if you maintained, imperfectly but consistently, the limits you have been working on in this book?

Your Chapter 18 Practice

This week, do a consistency audit on one limit you have already set. Ask yourself honestly: is it still holding? Has it drifted in any way, exceptions that have become habits, softening that has become surrender?

If it is holding well, document that. Write down that it is holding and what you have been doing that is working. That record matters.

If it has drifted, do not judge it. Just name it. Where specifically has it slipped? What would returning to it look like this week? What is one specific thing you will do to recalibrate?

The long game is won in the weekly audit, not just the first conversation. Small corrections made early cost far less than large corrections made after the pattern has fully reasserted itself.

Chapter 19: When Your Limits Change You

Nobody warns you about this part.

They tell you that limits will help your relationships. That people will respect you more. That you will feel better about yourself. And sometimes all of that is true.

But what they do not always tell you is that setting and holding limits consistently, really doing this work over time, changes you in ways that go beyond the relationships themselves. It changes how you see yourself. It changes what you are willing to accept. It changes, in some cases, who you are willing to be around.

And that change, even when it is good, comes with its own complexity. Some relationships will survive it and become richer. Others will not survive it at all. Your sense of who you are will shift. The version of you that existed before, the accommodating, endlessly available, conflict-avoiding version, will become harder to return to. And at some point you will realize you do not want to return to it.

This chapter is about that transformation. What it looks like, what it asks of you, and how to move through it with your eyes open.

The Identity Shift

People-pleasers often have a very specific self-concept. They are the helper, the peacekeeper, the one who holds things together, the person everyone can count on. That identity has been built over years, sometimes decades, and it comes with real rewards: appreciation, belonging, and the sense of being needed and valued.

When you begin to set limits, that identity comes under pressure. You are no longer always available. You are no longer always agreeable. You are no longer the person who absorbs whatever is handed to you without complaint.

And for a while, that can feel like loss. Like you are becoming someone worse, less caring, less generous, less good, rather than someone better.

Here is the reframe that matters: you are not becoming less caring. You are becoming more honest. The care you expressed before was often performed, driven by fear of consequences rather than genuine desire. The care you are capable of now, expressed from a place of genuine choice, is more real. It costs you something to give it. Which means when you give it, it actually means something.

The identity that is emerging is not smaller than the one it is replacing. It is truer. It is the version of you that shows up as yourself rather than as whoever everyone needs you to be.

The Relationships That Grow

Not all relationships suffer when you begin to hold limits. Some, often the ones you would least expect, actually deepen.

These are the relationships where the other person was never asking you to be limitless. They were engaging with whoever showed up and adjusting as you changed. When you become more honest, more willing to say what you actually think, decline what you do not want, and show up with your actual self, they find themselves in a richer relationship. Because they are finally talking to you rather than to the performance of you.

Partners who were unknowingly in a relationship with a performing people pleaser sometimes discover that the real person underneath is someone they like even more. Friends who sensed the inauthenticity but could not name it feel the relationship become more genuine. Family members who genuinely love you, not just the accommodating version of you, adjust and find they prefer the honest version.

These relationships are worth paying attention to. They are the evidence that limits do not destroy connection. They make it possible.

The Relationships That Struggle

Other relationships will struggle when you change. Some will struggle and then stabilize as the other person adjusts. Others will not recover.

The relationships most likely to struggle are the ones that were built, consciously or not, on the foundation of your limitlessness. Where the dynamic worked precisely because you absorbed, accommodated, and never pushed back. When you stop being that person, the foundation shifts and the relationship has to find a new one.

Some will. The other person will recognize that a relationship with the real you, even with its limits, is better than the arrangement they had with your performing self.

Others will not. They wanted access to the version of you that had no needs and caused no friction. That version is no longer available. When they realize this, they may leave, explicitly or by slowly withdrawing. Or you may realize that what they were offering was never what you wanted and make the decision yourself.

Both are honest outcomes. Neither is a failure.

Grieving Who You Used to Be

Here is something unexpected that often happens in this work: grief for the old self.

Not grief for the people-pleasing pattern, that you can let go of gladly. But grief for the version of yourself that existed within it.

The person who was always needed. The person who belonged everywhere because they offended no one.

When you change, that belonging shifts. You are no longer automatically welcome everywhere. You are no longer the person who fits into every situation because you have made yourself fit. You are a person with preferences, limits, and edges, and not every space will accommodate that.

That loss is real. Let yourself feel it without letting it pull you back. What you are trading is belonging through performance for belonging through authenticity. The second kind is rarer and harder to find. It is also the only kind that actually nourishes you.

Who You Are Becoming

The person on the other side of this work, the version of you that has genuinely internalized the right to take up space, have limits, and show up as yourself, is not a harder or colder person.

The reality is the opposite. People who have genuinely done this work are often warmer, not colder, because their warmth is no longer diluted by resentment. They are more generous, not less, because their generosity comes from actual desire rather than obligation. They are more present in their relationships because they are actually there, not monitoring everyone's needs and managing everyone's reactions.

What falls away is the performance. What remains is you.

And you, without the people-pleasing armor, without the compulsive accommodation, without the constant monitoring and managing, are someone worth knowing. Someone whose yes means something because their no is real. Someone whose presence in a room is genuine because they chose to be there.

That is who you are becoming. Keep going.

Navigating the Transition With People Who Knew the Old You

One of the specific challenges of this work is that most of the people you are changing in relationship with knew the old version of you. They have expectations based on who you were. When you change, they do not always have a framework for it.

Some will ask what is wrong with you. Some will suggest you have changed for the worse. Some will wonder aloud if you are angry, going through something, or have been influenced by someone who has turned you against them.

You do not owe them an explanation of your entire inner transformation. But you can offer something simple and honest:

I am working on being more honest about what I need. It might look different from how I have been before. I am still the same person. I am just trying to show up more genuinely.

That is enough. You do not have to justify growth. You do not have to get their approval for becoming more yourself.

The New Relationships You Attract

As you change, you will begin to attract different people, or notice differently the people who were always there.

People who have their own healthy limits recognize them in others. They do not need you to be endlessly available because they are not endlessly available themselves. They respect your no because they have their own. They show up for the real you because that is who they are interested in.

The relationships you build from this version of yourself, the one with genuine limits and genuine presence, will be different from the ones you built as a people pleaser. They will be fewer, perhaps.

You will no longer be everyone's person. But they will be more real. And real, in the end, is the only thing that sustains you.

The Changes That Surprise You

Some of the ways that limits will change you are predictable. You expect to feel less resentful. You expect your relationships to shift. You expect to feel more like yourself.

But some of the changes come as genuine surprises.

You may find that you have opinions about things you thought you did not care about. Preferences that went underground years ago because expressing them caused friction surface again, tentatively at first, and then with more confidence. You discover that you actually do care where you go for dinner, what you do on weekends, and how you spend your time. The caring was always there. It just learned to stay quiet.

You may find that the relationships you thought were your closest feel less central, while some you dismissed as peripheral reveal unexpected depth. The people who show up for the real you are not always the ones you expected.

You may find that you are less afraid. Not fearless, but less reflexively braced for the consequences of taking up space. The feared outcomes that drove years of self-erasure turn out to be less catastrophic than you believed. And that discovery, quiet and accumulating, is one of the most significant things this work produces.

You are becoming someone new. Give yourself the grace to not know yet exactly who that person is.

Reflection Questions

How has your sense of who you are already shifted since you began working on limits? What feels different about how you see yourself?

Which of your current relationships do you think will grow as you continue this work? What makes you believe they are capable of that?

Which relationships do you fear might not survive the change? How do you feel about that, honestly?

Is there grief for the old version of yourself, the accommodating, always-available one, mixed in with your relief at changing? What do you miss about that version, if anything?

Who is the person you are becoming? Describe them in a few sentences. What do they value? How do they show up? What do they no longer do?

Your Chapter 19 Practice

This week, write a short letter to the version of yourself that existed before you began this work. Not to criticize them. They were doing the best they could with what they had. But to acknowledge them, honor what they were carrying, and tell them what you are building now.

Tell them what you know now that they did not. Tell them what you have learned about what it costs to disappear. Tell them where you are going.

This is a way of completing the transition with compassion, of honoring the journey without staying in the old place. The letter is for you. You never have to show it to anyone.

Chapter 20: Boundaries and Belonging

The deepest fear underneath people-pleasing is not really about conflict or disapproval. It is about belonging.

The fear is this: if I have limits, if I say no, if I stop being endlessly available and agreeable, I will end up alone. The people I love will leave. The community I have built around my usefulness will dissolve. I will lose my place.

That fear is real. It has roots. For many people pleasers it was confirmed early: a parent who withdrew when they were not compliant, a friendship group that only wanted them when they were useful, or a relationship where love felt conditional on accommodation. The lesson got written deep: belonging requires self-erasure.

This chapter challenges that belief directly. Not by dismissing the fear, because it deserves to be taken seriously, but by examining what genuine belonging actually requires and what kind of belonging is actually worth having.

Two Kinds of Belonging

There is belonging that comes from being needed, and there is belonging that comes from being known.

Belonging through being needed is what most people pleasers have spent their lives cultivating. You are included because you are useful. You are invited because you say yes. You are kept because you do not cause trouble. Your place in the group is contingent on your continued performance of availability and accommodation.

This kind of belonging is real, but it is conditional. And the condition, your ongoing self-erasure, is one you can never fully meet, because it requires you to have no limits, no bad days, and no moments of genuine need. The moment you do have those things, the belonging wobbles.

Belonging through being known is different. It does not require performance. It requires presence: showing up as yourself, with your actual thoughts, preferences, and limits, and being accepted in that form. It is rarer and harder to find. It cannot be manufactured by making yourself useful enough.

The tragedy of people-pleasing is that in pursuing the first kind of belonging, you make the second kind impossible. You cannot be known if you are always performing. You cannot be genuinely loved if no one can see who you actually are.

Why Real Belonging Requires Limits

Here is the paradox that sits at the heart of this book: limits do not threaten belonging. They make genuine belonging possible.

Genuine connection requires two things: authenticity and trust. Authenticity means showing up as your actual self, your preferences, your limits, and your honest reactions. Trust means knowing that the other person will still be there when you do.

When you have no limits, you cannot offer authenticity because you are performing. And when the other person has never had to accept your no, they have never had the opportunity to demonstrate that they will. The relationship exists in a kind of manufactured safety that has not been tested.

When you set a limit and someone accepts it, when you say no and they stay, when you disappoint them and they are still there the next day, that is the moment genuine trust becomes possible. Because now you know: this person wants you, not just your accommodation.

Limits are, in this sense, the test of real connection. Not a test you administer deliberately, but a natural sorting that happens when you start showing up honestly. The people who stay when you show up honestly are the ones who were actually there for you.

Building Community Around Authenticity

People pleasers are often excellent at building large networks of surface connections and terrible at building small circles of genuine ones. They are everyone's acquaintance and no one's real friend because real friendship requires the kind of honesty and self-disclosure that people-pleasing makes dangerous.

Shifting from surface connections to genuine ones requires being willing to disagree. Real friends disagree. They have different opinions and they say so. They push back on each other's thinking. They tolerate being told they are wrong without the relationship fracturing. If you have never disagreed with someone, you do not have a relationship with them. You have a performance reviewed by an audience.

It requires showing your actual needs. People pleasers are often much better at meeting needs than at having them. They show up when others are struggling and disappear when they are struggling themselves.

Genuine community requires reciprocity. You need to be able to say: I am not doing well. I need something. Can you help me? That vulnerability, the willingness to be the person who needs something rather than the person who provides it, is what allows real closeness to form.

It requires letting people know you. Genuine belonging requires disclosure. Not oversharing, not dumping your interior life on everyone you meet, but the gradual, mutual exchange of real thoughts and experiences that constitutes actually knowing another person. When you let someone know you, and they choose to stay, that is belonging.

Accepting that not everyone will stay is also part of this work. Building a life of genuine connection means accepting that not everyone will be part of it. Some people wanted the performing version of you and will not adjust to the real one. That loss is real. But what is on the other side of it is the possibility of connections that do not require you to disappear. And that possibility is worth the loss of connections that required exactly that.

The Myth That Limits Make You Selfish

The accusation that stops many people in their tracks when they begin this work is the word selfish. That having limits is selfish. That saying no is selfish. That putting your own needs anywhere in the picture is selfish.

It is worth examining this directly.

Selfishness is the excessive prioritization of your own needs at the expense of others. It is real. It is worth guarding against. But that is not what limits are.

A limit is not I come first, you do not matter. A limit is I matter too. Those are not the same statement.

You can have limits and still be generous. You can say no to some things and yes to others. You can protect your energy and still show up fully for the people and causes that matter to you. In fact, limits make that kind of genuine generosity possible because when you are not giving from depletion, you are giving from abundance. And what comes from abundance is qualitatively different from what comes from the bottom of an empty well.

The people who call your limits selfish are often the people who benefited most from your limitlessness. Their accusation is not an objective assessment. It is the protest of someone who is losing access to something they were accustomed to having.

Take it seriously enough to examine it. But do not let it be the final word.

What Genuine Belonging Feels Like

Many people-pleasers have never experienced genuine belonging, or experienced it so briefly that they have forgotten what it feels like. Here is what it looks like when it is real.

You do not have to manage your energy before spending time with these people. You leave feeling restored rather than depleted.

You can say no without the relationship going cold. Disappointing them is uncomfortable but survivable, for both of you.

You can share what you are actually thinking without editing it into the version they want to hear.

You do not monitor their mood and adjust your behavior accordingly. You can be in a bad mood yourself without feeling like you have broken something.

They show up for you. Not just when it is convenient. Not just when you are useful. But when you need something.

You feel like yourself around them. Not a better version of yourself, not a performance of yourself. Just yourself.

If none of your current relationships feel this way, that is important information. Not a reason to despair. Many people who have spent years in people-pleasing mode have to rebuild their social world as they change. But it is a reason to keep going, because what you are working toward is exactly this.

The Life That Becomes Possible

Here is what becomes possible when you stop choosing between connection and self-respect.

You can be fully present in your relationships because you are not spending half your attention monitoring everyone's reactions and managing your own presentation. You are just there.

You can give generously because you are giving from choice rather than obligation. Your yes means something because your no is real.

You can ask for help without it costing you the identity of being the helper. You can be vulnerable without it being a liability.

You can love people honestly, telling them the truth, including hard truths, because the relationship is strong enough to hold it.

And you can belong to communities, relationships, and spaces as yourself: not as the role you have been playing, not as the function you serve, but as the person you actually are.

That is not a small thing. For many people who have spent years disappearing into other people's needs and expectations, it is everything.

Reflection Questions

Which of your current relationships feel like belonging through being known rather than belonging through being needed? What makes them feel different?

Have you ever let someone know you, shared something real about yourself, and had them respond in a way that built genuine trust? What happened?

Where in your life have you been pursuing belonging through performance, and what has it cost you?

Is there a community, friendship, or relationship you have avoided deepening because you were not sure who you would be in it if you stopped performing? What would it look like to show up more genuinely there?

What would your social world look like if it were built entirely around people who accepted you with your limits?

Your Chapter 20 Practice

This week, in one relationship that matters to you, practice one small act of genuine self-disclosure. Not a dramatic revelation. Just something true. A real opinion. An honest reaction. A preference you would normally swallow. A no to something small that you would normally absorb.

Then notice what happens. Not just how they respond, but how you feel. Whether being known, even slightly more than before, feels different from being needed.

Genuine belonging is built in increments. This week's increment is one honest moment in one relationship. That is enough.

PART FIVE

Living Boundary-Forward

Chapter 21: The Generous Life

There is a version of generosity that depletes you. That asks everything and restores nothing. That gives until the well is dry and then asks why you are tired all the time.

Most people-pleasers know this version intimately. They have been endlessly, automatically, compulsively generous in this way for years. And they have paid for it in exhaustion, resentment, diminishment, and the slow erasure of the self that was supposed to be doing the giving.

This chapter is about a different kind of generosity. The kind that comes from fullness rather than depletion. The kind that is given by choice rather than obligation. The kind that is sustainable over a lifetime because it is rooted in genuine desire rather than fear of what happens if you stop.

This kind of generosity is only possible when you have limits. Not despite them. Because of them.

The Difference Between Compulsive Giving and Genuine Generosity

They can look identical from the outside. Someone who gives compulsively and someone who gives genuinely may perform the same acts: the same favor granted, the same time offered, and the same support provided. The difference is what is happening underneath.

Compulsive giving happens because saying no feels dangerous. It is driven by the need to be needed, to be liked, and to maintain your place. It comes with a silent ledger, a tracking of what you have given that you are not supposed to acknowledge but cannot help keeping. It produces resentment over time because you are giving what you did not freely choose to give. It leaves you depleted because there is no built-in replenishment.

Genuine generosity happens because you genuinely want to, because giving in this instance brings you real satisfaction. It is chosen, not compelled. You could say no. You are saying yes because you want to. It comes without a ledger. You give and release. It produces a different feeling in your body: warmth, connection, and the quiet satisfaction of having done something that mattered.

The path from the first kind to the second runs directly through limits. When you stop giving out of obligation, what remains is what you actually want to give. And what you actually want to give, given from fullness, is infinitely more valuable than what you gave because you could not say no.

There is a specific kind of exhaustion that comes from compulsive giving that is different from ordinary tiredness. It is the exhaustion of someone who has been giving something away that was not freely offered. The fatigue is real, but underneath it is something else: a low-grade resentment that has no clean object because you agreed to everything. You said yes. It was your choice.

Except it was not really a choice, not in the meaningful sense. A choice requires a genuine alternative. And for most people pleasers, no never felt like a genuine alternative. It felt like a threat. To the relationship, to the other person's approval, and to your own sense of being a good person.

So you gave, and kept giving, and called it generosity. But generosity given under duress is not generosity. It is compliance dressed in generous clothing. And the body knows the difference, even when the mind does not. The resentment is the signal. Genuine giving does not produce resentment. It produces, at most, a mild tiredness and, underneath that, the quiet satisfaction of having given something freely.

The goal of this chapter is not to make you give less. It is to make what you give genuine.

The Full Cup Principle

You have probably heard some version of this: you cannot pour from an empty cup. It has been printed on enough coffee mugs that it is easy to dismiss. But it is true, and most people pleasers have not actually applied it to their lives.

Your energy, attention, emotional capacity, time, and financial resources are finite. Not as a character flaw or a personal failing, but as a fact of being human. You have a limit to how much of these things you can give before you need to replenish.

When you give without replenishing, when the outflow consistently exceeds the inflow, you eventually have nothing of quality left to give. You become the person who shows up for others but is barely present. Who says yes but does it hollow. Who gives time and energy that is thin and strained rather than full and nourishing.

The limits you set are not walls that keep your generosity in. They are the management of your resources so that your generosity remains genuine. When you say no to one thing, you are preserving the capacity to say a real yes to another.

Giving From Choice

The test of genuine generosity is simple: could you have said no?

When the answer is yes, when you had a real choice and you chose to give, the giving lands differently. The person receiving it can feel the difference, even if they cannot name it. There is something qualitatively different about receiving from someone who chose to give versus receiving from someone who could not say no.

This is why your yes becomes more meaningful when your no is real. The people in your life learn, through experience over time, that when you say yes, you mean it. That your presence is chosen. That your help is offered from genuine desire, not from the inability to refuse.

What You Can Give When You Are Not Exhausted

When you stop giving from depletion, several things become available.

Presence. When you are not running on empty, you can actually be there, not going through the motions of being there while your mind is on everything you have not done for yourself.

Quality attention. The difference between half-hearted help and full-hearted help is significant. When you have capacity, you can bring your whole self to what you are doing for someone else.

Patience. Depletion produces irritability. Fullness produces patience. The parent who has had nothing for themselves all week is a different parent than the one who has had a few hours to restore.

Joy. The ability to celebrate someone else's good news, to be genuinely happy for them, and to take pleasure in their success. These come much more easily when you are not running a deficit.

Generosity Toward Yourself

One of the forms of generosity that people pleasers are worst at is generosity toward themselves. They extend enormous charity to others: patience, understanding, and the benefit of the doubt, along with second and third and fourth chances. And they offer almost none of it to themselves.

They hold themselves to standards they would never apply to someone they love. They speak to themselves in tones they would never accept from another person.

Self-generosity is not self-indulgence. It is the application of the same basic compassion you extend to others to the person who arguably needs it most: you.

Rest without justification. Resting because you are tired, not because you have earned it through sufficient productivity.

Pleasure without guilt. Doing things you enjoy because enjoyment matters, not because you have done enough to deserve it.

Mistakes without self-punishment. Acknowledging what went wrong, learning from it, and moving on.

Needs without apology. Having needs and meeting them without treating them as impositions on the world.

When you are generous with yourself, you are not taking from others. You are building the reserves that make genuine generosity toward others possible.

The Most Generous Thing You Can Do

Here is the most important thing in this chapter: the most generous thing you can do for the people you love is to show up as yourself.

Not as the performing version of yourself that absorbs and accommodates and never has needs. Not as the depleted version that shows up physically but is absent in every way that matters. As yourself, with your genuine reactions, your honest preferences, your real capacity on any given day, and your limits.

Because when you show up as yourself, the people you love get to have a real relationship with a real person. They get to know you. They get to rely on the version of you that is actually there rather than the performance that could collapse at any moment. They get the full version, the one that has genuine warmth because it has not been performing warmth for so long that the genuine article got lost.

That is a gift. An enormous one. And it requires limits to give.

Reflection Questions

Think of something you give, time, help, emotional support, or attention, that you give compulsively rather than by genuine choice. What would it feel like to give that same thing from choice instead?

When did you last feel genuinely replenished, not just rested, but restored? What were the conditions? How long ago was it?

Is there someone in your life who gives generously from what seems like a genuine place rather than obligation? What does their giving feel like to receive?

How do you treat yourself when you make a mistake or fall short? Would you treat someone you love that way?

What would become available to you, what would you be able to give and to whom, if you were not chronically running on empty?

Your Chapter 21 Practice

This week, identify one way you have been giving from depletion, one area where your giving has become automatic and obligatory rather than chosen and genuine.

Then do one thing to replenish in that area. Not a dramatic overhaul. One specific act of restoration. Take the morning you have been giving away. Say no to the request that comes from habit rather than genuine desire. Do the thing that restores you that you have been postponing because it felt selfish.

Notice what it feels like to give yourself something. Notice whether it actually makes the other things you give more genuine.

The generous life is not the life of endless giving. It is the life of giving well, from fullness, by choice, with your whole self present. Building that life starts with this: treating your own restoration as something that matters.

Chapter 22: Teaching Others Through Your Example

You are not setting limits in a vacuum. You are setting them inside a web of relationships, with people who are watching, learning, and being shaped by what they see you do.

This is especially true if you are a parent, a manager, a teacher, an older sibling, or anyone else whose behavior carries particular weight for those who look up to you. But it is true even in ordinary adult relationships. What we do in the presence of others teaches them what is normal, possible, and acceptable.

The people-pleasers in your life learned their patterns somewhere. From parents who never said no. From communities that equated self-sacrifice with virtue. From relationships that rewarded compliance and punished honesty. The model they were given shaped what they believed was available to them.

You are now becoming a different model. That matters more than you may realize.

How We Learn What Is Possible

Most of what we know about how to be in relationships was not taught to us explicitly. It was absorbed. We watched the people around us, how they handled conflict, how they responded to requests, and what they did when they were tired, overwhelmed, or pushed past their limit, and we absorbed it as the way things work.

If you watched adults around you absorb everything without complaint, you absorbed the message that that is what adults do. If you watched people give until they collapsed and then be praised for their sacrifice, you absorbed the message that sacrifice is love. If you never saw anyone in your world hold a limit without apologizing for it, you absorbed the message that limits require apology.

You are now doing something different. And the people watching you are absorbing that too.

What Children Learn From Your Limits

Children who watch a parent hold limits with dignity learn things that cannot be taught through words alone. That adults have needs, and that having need is normal. That it is possible to love someone and still say no to them. That rest, time alone, and personal space are legitimate needs, not signs of failure. That saying no does not destroy relationships. That self-respect and kindness are not opposites.

Children who watch a parent with no limits learn the opposite of all of these things. They learn that adults exist to serve other people's needs. That love requires self-erasure. That saying no is dangerous.

Those lessons become the blueprint for how they navigate their own adult relationships. Not because they chose them, but because they absorbed them from watching the most influential people in their early lives.

What you model now is part of what they will carry. That is not pressure. It is simply the truth about how this works.

The Modeling Effect Among Equals

When you say no to something in a group of people who have never heard you say no, something shifts in the room. The silence after your no is not just your discomfort. It is also the moment when the people around you recalibrate what they thought was possible.

Oh. She said no. And she did not apologize. And the world did not end.

That moment is permission. Not explicit permission. But the implicit permission of seeing it done. Of watching someone hold a limit without crumbling and survive to tell the tale.

This is particularly powerful in contexts where people-pleasing is the norm: workplaces where everyone stays late because no one leaves on time, friendships where no one ever declines an invitation, and families where no one ever pushes back on anything. In those environments, your limit is not just a personal act. It is a demonstration of possibility.

The Difference Between Modeling and Preaching

Modeling is not the same as telling people what they should do.

The most powerful teaching happens not when you explain your limits to others or encourage them to develop their own, but when you simply live your limits in front of them without comment. The less you explain it, the more powerful it tends to be.

People who are ready to see it will see it. They will watch you hold a limit under pressure and file that away. They will see you say no to something they have never been able to say no to and feel something shift. They will watch you survive the discomfort of disappointing someone and notice that you are still standing.

They may not mention it. They may not even consciously register it as significant in the moment. But it will have landed. And at some point in their own life, when they are in a situation that calls for the thing they watched you do, they will have a reference point they did not have before.

You do not have to be an evangelist for limits. You just have to live them.

When Someone You Care About Is Struggling

Because you are doing this work, people in your life may begin to bring their own struggles to you. A friend who is exhausted from over-giving. A family member who cannot say no. A colleague who is drowning in obligations they did not choose.

Listen before advising. The first thing someone needs when they are struggling is to be heard, not fixed. Resist the urge to immediately share everything you have learned.

Share from your own experience, not as instruction. The most useful thing you can offer is your own story: what it was like before, what you tried, what happened, what it costs, and what it gives. Not here is what you should do, but here is what I have been working on.

Do not rescue them from their process. It can be painful to watch someone you care about struggle with something you have worked hard to understand. The impulse to solve it for them is a loving impulse that ultimately does not serve them. Growth happens through the struggle. They need to find their own relationship with their limits in their own time.

Breaking the Chain

People-pleasing patterns are often generational. They pass from parent to child, from culture to community member, and from one relationship to the next. Not because anyone chose to transmit them, but because they were lived in front of people who had no other model.

When you do this work, genuinely, imperfectly, over time, you break a link in that chain. The patterns that were passed to you do not have to be passed forward in the same form. The people watching you get a different model. The children in your life get a different blueprint.

This is not a small thing. Generational patterns are stubborn. They persist not because they serve people well, but because no one in the line has had the tools or the permission to do anything different.

You now have both. The work you do on yourself ripples outward in ways you may never fully see or know. But they are real.

When Someone in Your Life Is Learning

Because you are doing this work, people in your life may begin to bring their own struggles to you. A friend who is exhausted from over-giving. A family member who cannot say no. A colleague who is drowning in obligations they did not choose.

Here is how to be genuinely useful without overstepping.

Listen before advising. The first thing someone needs when they are struggling is to be heard, not fixed. Resist the urge to immediately share everything you have learned. Ask questions. Reflect back what you are hearing. Let them come to their own clarity before you offer anything.

Share from your own experience, not as instruction. The most useful thing you can offer is your own story: what it was like before, what you tried, what happened, what it costs, and what it gives. Not here is what you should do, but here is what I have been working on.

Do not rescue them from their process. It can be painful to watch someone you care about struggle with something you have worked hard to understand. But growth happens through the struggle. They need to find their own relationship with their limits in their own time. You can walk alongside that process. You cannot do it for them.

Be the proof that it is possible. More than anything you can say, the fact of your own changed life is the most useful thing you offer.

You are living proof that it is possible to change this pattern, have limits, hold them, and build a life that does not require your disappearance.

Reflection Questions

Who is watching you, children, younger colleagues, friends, or siblings, who might be absorbing your patterns of giving and limiting? What are they learning from what they see?

Think of someone whose limits you admire. What specifically did watching them teach you that you could not have learned from being told?

Has anyone in your life started to change their own patterns since you have been changing yours? Have you noticed any ripple effects you did not expect?

Is there someone in your life who is struggling with people-pleasing that you have been wanting to help? What would it look like to support them without trying to fix them?

What generational pattern around self-sacrifice or limitlessness did you inherit? What would it mean to be the person in your family line who changed it?

Your Chapter 22 Practice

This week, be intentional about one visible limit. Not for the sake of performance, not to teach anyone a lesson, but simply as your own genuine act, in the presence of others, without comment or explanation.

Hold the limit the same way you would if no one were watching. Let the fact of it be enough.

Then notice: did anyone see? Did anything shift, in the room, in the relationship, or in the way someone looked at you after?

You may never know the full effect of what you are modeling. Most of it will be invisible. But it is happening. And it is part of what makes this work worth doing beyond yourself.

Chapter 23: When It Is Hard

This chapter is for the days when you know everything in this book and still cannot make yourself do it.

The days when the guilt is louder than your clarity. When someone pushes back and you feel yourself folding, even as part of you knows you should not. When you are tired and depleted and the path of least resistance is just to give in, and the version of you that knows better is simply not loud enough to compete.

Those days are real. They happen to everyone doing this work, at every stage of the process. They do not mean you have failed. They do not mean you will never change. They mean you are human, this is hard, and the patterns you are working against are older and deeper than the new ones you are building.

This chapter will not make those days disappear. It will give you something to reach for when they arrive.

Why Some Days Are Harder Than Others

Not all hard days are created equal. Understanding which kind of hard day you are having helps you choose the right response.

The Depletion Day

You have not slept enough. You have been giving too much for too long. You are running on empty and every interaction requires more than you have. On depletion days, holding a limit feels like an enormous act of willpower because it is. You are trying to do something effortful from a place of no resources.

The response to a depletion day is not to push through with grit. It is to do whatever small thing restores even a fragment of capacity. Thirty minutes alone. A walk. Food that is not eaten standing over the sink. The barest minimum of restoration that allows you to function.

Lower your expectations for what you will hold today. Pick the one limit that matters most and let the smaller ones go. You are not failing by being human. You are being realistic about what you have.

The High-Stakes Day

Today is the day you have to have the hard conversation. Or the person most likely to make you crumble is the one making the request. Or the stakes are high enough that the usual discomfort of holding a limit is amplified by the weight of what might be lost.

High-stakes days call for preparation, not just willpower. Have your language ready in advance. Know what you are going to say. Have thought through the most likely pushback and how you will respond. The moment itself is not the time to be figuring things out. It is the time to reach for what you have already prepared.

And know this: the high-stakes days are the ones that matter most. They are the moments that either erode the work you have been doing or cement it. Holding a limit in a high-stakes moment teaches your nervous system something that ten easy moments cannot.

The Grief Day

Today you are not struggling with willpower. You are struggling with sadness. Maybe you held a limit and the relationship shifted in a way you did not want. Maybe you are accepting something about a person you love that is painful to accept. Maybe you are mourning the old version of yourself or the relationships that did not survive your change.

Grief days do not call for action. They call for sitting with what is. You do not have to fix the sadness, resolve it, or move past it quickly. Let it be there. The grief is part of the work, not an interruption of it.

The Doubt Day

Today the voice that says maybe you are wrong is louder than usual. Maybe you are being too rigid. Maybe the people who say you have changed for the worse are right. Maybe the old way was better. At least everyone was happier, even if you were not.

Doubt days are normal. They do not require urgent action. They require honesty. Ask yourself: is there new information here, or is this just the old pattern trying to reassert itself? Write down what you know to be true. Not what you feel today, but what you know. Feelings fluctuate. The knowledge of what things were like before, why you started this work, and what it cost you not to do it, that is more stable than today's doubt.

The Minimum Viable Limit

On hard days, perfection is not the goal. The goal is the minimum viable limit, the smallest, most achievable version of holding your ground that keeps the pattern moving in the right direction.

You do not have to have the full conversation today. You just have to not say yes to the thing you were going to say yes to.

You do not have to address the larger pattern today. You just have to not absorb this specific instance of it.

You do not have to be the fully formed person you are becoming today. You just have to take one step in that direction instead of one step backward.

The minimum viable limit is still a limit. It counts. It keeps the thread of the pattern running in the right direction even when you cannot do more than that.

What to Say to Yourself on Hard Days

The internal voice on hard days is often not helpful. It catastrophizes, criticizes, and replays the worst-case scenarios. It needs something to push against.

Here are the things worth saying back:

This is hard because it is new. Hard and wrong are not the same thing.

I have felt this way before and held anyway. I can do it again.

The discomfort I feel right now is the feeling of doing something important.

I do not have to do this perfectly. I just have to do something.

The version of me on the other side of this moment is someone I respect. I am building toward that person right now.

I am allowed to need time. I am allowed to be imperfect. I am not allowed to give up on myself.

These are not affirmations in the hollow sense. They are true statements you can return to when the doubt is loud. The practice of saying them, especially when they feel slightly out of reach, is itself part of building the self-trust that makes the hard days less hard over time.

Asking for Help

One of the most consistent patterns among people pleasers is the inability to ask for help. They are much better at being the helper than being the person who needs something.

Hard days are when this pattern most needs to be broken.

You are allowed, genuinely allowed, to reach out to someone you trust and say: today is hard. I am struggling to hold something I know I need to hold. Can you help me think through it? Can you just be a presence while I work through this?

That ask is not weakness. It is the application of genuine connection to the moments that need it most. And it models, for yourself, that asking for support is part of what strong people do, not a departure from strength.

When You Have Already Given In

The chapter on consistency covered this, but it bears repeating: if you have already given in today, the day is not lost.

You gave in. That happened. It does not erase every limit you have held. It does not prove you will never change. It is one instance of the old pattern in a life that is otherwise moving in a different direction.

What you do after giving in matters more than the giving in itself. You can spiral into self-criticism, which will make the next instance more likely. Or you can notice it, understand what happened, and return to the path without making the slip the whole story.

The return is available to you. Always. However many times you need it.

Remembering Why

On the hardest days, when the reasons you started this work feel abstract and the cost of continuing feels very concrete, go back to why.

Not the intellectual why. The felt why. The memory of what it was like before. The exhaustion of constantly managing everyone else's experience. The resentment that built in silence. The slow disappearance of the self you were supposed to be living as.

Remember the moment you decided something had to change. Not as a source of pain, but as an anchor. That moment was true. The person who made that decision knew something important. When today's hard day is trying to talk you out of the work, that person is the one worth listening to.

You started this for real reasons. Those reasons do not disappear on the hard days. They are still there, waiting for you to remember them.

Reflection Questions

Which kind of hard day do you have most often, depletion, high-stakes, grief, or doubt? What does it look and feel like for you specifically?

What is your minimum viable limit, the smallest, most achievable version of holding your ground, for the situation currently hardest for you?

What do you say to yourself on hard days that makes things worse? What could you say instead?

Is there someone you could reach out to on a hard day, someone who would understand what you are working on and be genuinely helpful?

What was the moment, the specific experience or realization, that made you decide something had to change? Can you hold that memory clearly enough to return to it on hard days?

Your Chapter 23 Practice

This week, prepare for your next hard day before it arrives.

Write down three things: the limit you are most likely to struggle with, the specific situation most likely to make you want to give in, and the one sentence you will say to yourself in that moment when everything in you wants to fold.

Put it somewhere you will actually find it. Your phone. A notebook. A sticky note in the right place. The preparation is not a guarantee. But it changes the odds. When you arrive at the hard moment already knowing what you are going to do, the decision has already been made. You just have to follow through.

Hard days are not the exception. They are part of the practice. And the people who change, the ones who actually build the life they want, are not the ones who only show up on the easy days. They are the ones who show up on the hard ones too.

Chapter 24: Your Boundary Blueprint

You have spent twenty-three chapters building understanding, language, and practice. You know what people-pleasing is and where it comes from. You know how to communicate a limit, how to handle pushback, how to follow through on consequences, and how to manage guilt. You know what self-respect looks like as a daily practice and what genuine generosity feels like from the inside.

Now it is time to put it together into something personal. Not a generic set of principles, but a blueprint that is yours, specific to your life, your relationships, your history, and the particular shape of your people-pleasing.

This chapter is a working chapter. It asks more of you than any other because it asks you to be specific. Not about limits in the abstract, but about your limits. Not about relationships in general, but about your relationships. Not about who you want to become eventually, but about what that means right now, in the life you are actually living.

Take your time with this one. Write in the margins. Come back to it. Let it be a document you return to and revise as your life changes and your practice deepens.

Part One: Taking Stock

Before you can move forward, you need to see clearly where you are. Answer the following questions as honestly as you can.

Where are you currently operating without limits? List every area of your life where you consistently give more than you have, say yes when you mean no, or absorb things you should not absorb. Be specific. Not at work, but I respond to emails at midnight because I am afraid of what my manager will think if I do not. Not in my marriage, but I never say I am tired because I am afraid my partner will feel neglected.

What are you most resentful about right now? Resentment is a signal. It points to the places where you have been giving without choice, absorbing without limit, and accommodating without reciprocation. List what you are resentful about without editing it for fairness or reasonableness. The list itself is information.

What have you been tolerating that you know you should not? Not what someone else would say you should not tolerate. What do you know, in your own honest assessment, has been going on too long without being addressed?

Where do you feel most like yourself? The places, relationships, and contexts where you do not have to perform, where you show up as your actual self and feel accepted in that form. These are your reference points for what genuine belonging feels like.

What do you want more of? Not what you think you should want. Not what would make others happy. What do you actually want more of in your life? Time alone. Genuine connection. Creative work. Rest. Purpose. Name it honestly.

Part Two: Your Priority Limits

Based on your honest assessment, identify the three to five limits that matter most right now. Not every limit you will ever need, just the ones that are most urgent, most overdue, and most necessary for your wellbeing.

For each one, answer these questions.

The limit. State it in one clear sentence. What specifically will you no longer accept, or what specifically will you start requiring?

The relationship or context. Who is this with, and in what setting? Be specific. Better limits with family is not a limit. I will not stay on a call with my mother when she begins criticizing my parenting is.

Why it matters. What has it cost you not to have this limit? Write this in felt terms. Not it affects my wellbeing, but I spend every Sunday dreading Monday because I know I will absorb whatever comes and never say anything.

The consequence. If this limit is crossed, what will you do? State it specifically. Make sure it is something you will actually do.

The first step. What is the smallest, most concrete action you can take this week toward this limit? Not the full conversation. The first step. I will not respond to that text tonight. I will say I need to check my calendar before committing. I will leave the room the next time that subject comes up.

Part Three: Your Relationship Map

Look at your most significant relationships and place each one honestly in one of four categories.

Nourishing. Relationships where you feel genuinely seen, where the giving is roughly reciprocal, and where you can show up as yourself. These are the relationships to invest in and protect.

Workable. Relationships that matter but have patterns that need addressing. The limit conversations have not been had, or have been had partially, and there is genuine possibility if things shift. These are the relationships where your priority limits live.

Draining. Relationships that consistently cost more than they give, where your limits are not respected despite being stated, and where you feel worse after almost every interaction. These relationships need either significant change or significant distance.

Transitional. Relationships in the process of changing, either moving toward something healthier as you and the other person adjust, or moving toward an ending as the incompatibility becomes clearer. These relationships need honesty about which direction they are actually heading.

Once you have mapped your relationships, ask yourself: where is the majority of your time and energy going? Is it proportional to where the nourishment is coming from?

Part Four: Your Non-Negotiables

These are the limits that are not situational, not relationship-specific, and not subject to adjustment based on who is asking or how much pressure is applied. They are the floor, the minimum standards for how you will be treated that apply in every context.

Most people have somewhere between three and seven of these. They tend to cluster around dignity, honesty, and basic reciprocity.

I will not stay in conversations where I am being yelled at or spoken to with contempt.

I will not participate in relationships where my no is consistently treated as a negotiating position.

I will not give from depletion. When I have nothing left, I say so.

I will not apologize for having needs.

Write yours. Make them specific enough to be actionable and broad enough to apply across contexts.

Part Five: Your Daily Practice

From the practices in this book, identify three that you commit to maintaining.

One self-respect practice. Something from Chapter 17 that you will do consistently. Pick one. Commit to it.

One recovery practice. Something you will do when you slip. Write down exactly what you will do: notice it, write about it, call someone, and return to the limit at the next opportunity. Have the recovery planned in advance.

One replenishment practice. Something that restores you, scheduled into your life as a non-negotiable rather than a reward for sufficient productivity. It does not have to be elaborate. It has to be real and it has to happen.

Part Six: Your Six-Month Vision

Six months from now, if you have been working this blueprint, imperfectly, with setbacks, but consistently in the right direction, what is different?

Be specific. Not I will have better limits, but: which relationships have shifted? What are you no longer tolerating? What have you stopped doing out of obligation? What are you doing now that you chose rather than felt compelled to? What does a typical week look like?

Write this vision in the present tense, as if it is already true. Not I will, but I am. Not I hope to, but I do.

This is not magical thinking. It is target-setting. You cannot move toward a destination you have not named. Name it. Make it specific enough that you will know when you have arrived.

Returning to This Chapter

This blueprint is not a document you complete once and file away. It is a living reference, something to return to quarterly, something to revise as your circumstances change and your understanding deepens.

Six months from now, come back to it. See what has shifted. Update your relationship map. Revise your priority limits. Adjust your daily practices based on what has actually worked.

The blueprint is a snapshot of where you are and where you are going at a particular moment in your growth. It will change because you will change. The work is not to get the blueprint right once. It is to keep returning to it honestly.

Reflection Questions

What emerged from the taking stock section that surprised you, something you had not fully acknowledged to yourself before?

What is the one priority limit that, if you held it consistently for six months, would change the most about your daily life?

Looking at your relationship map, is there a relationship you have been mentally categorizing as workable that honest assessment would place in draining? What would that reclassification mean?

What are your non-negotiables? Have you written them down? If not, what has kept you from committing to them in writing?

What does your six-month vision feel like when you read it back? Does it feel possible, or does it feel like someone else's life?

Your Chapter 24 Practice

This week, complete at least Parts One and Two of this blueprint. You do not have to finish all six parts in one sitting. But taking stock and identifying your priority limits are the foundation. Start there.

Write it by hand if possible. There is something about the physical act of writing, the slower pace, and the permanence of ink that makes these commitments more real than typing them into a document that is easy to close and forget.

And then do the thing that will make this blueprint matter: share one piece of it with someone you trust. Not the whole thing. One priority limit. One non-negotiable. One honest acknowledgment of something you have been tolerating that you are committing to address.

Saying it to another person makes it real in a way that private writing alone does not. You are no longer someone who is thinking about changing. You are someone who has said, out loud, in the presence of another person, what you are building.

That is the beginning of accountability. And accountability is what turns a blueprint into a life.

Chapter 25: You Are Allowed

We have covered a great deal of ground together.

We have talked about where people-pleasing comes from and what it costs. We have worked through the mechanics of limits: how to set them, how to communicate them, how to hold them under pressure, and how to follow through when they are crossed. We have looked at guilt and pushback and consequences and grief. We have talked about self-respect, genuine generosity, belonging, and the long, slow work of becoming someone who shows up as themselves.

But before this book ends, there is something simpler that needs to be said.

Not a framework. Not a strategy. Just the truth, stated plainly, for the part of you that still needs to hear it.

You Are Allowed

You are allowed to take up space.

You are allowed to have needs.

You are allowed to be tired.

You are allowed to say no, to anyone, at any time, for any reason, or for no reason at all.

You are allowed to change your mind.

You are allowed to disappoint people.

You are allowed to not be available.

You are allowed to protect your time.

You are allowed to protect your energy.

You are allowed to protect your peace.

You are allowed to want things.

You are allowed to ask for what you want.

You are allowed to have preferences.

You are allowed to express those preferences without apologizing for them.

You are allowed to be angry.

You are allowed to be sad.

You are allowed to be struggling.

You are allowed to say so.

You are allowed to need help.

You are allowed to ask for it.

You are allowed to receive it without immediately trying to give something back.

You are allowed to leave a relationship that consistently harms you.

You are allowed to grieve that leaving.

You are allowed to build a different life on the other side of it.

You are allowed to love people and still have limits with them.

You are allowed to be kind and still say no.

You are allowed to be generous and still have lines you will not cross.

You are allowed to be a good person and still prioritize yourself.

You are allowed to show up imperfectly and keep going anyway.

You are allowed to change slowly.

You are allowed to change in ways that confuse people who knew the old you.

You are allowed to become someone the old you could not have imagined.

You are allowed to be yourself.

You are allowed to belong somewhere as yourself.

You are allowed to take your own life seriously.

None of this requires a particular set of circumstances. None of it requires that you first prove you have given enough, sacrificed enough, or been accommodating enough. It applies to you now, as you are, in the life you are actually living.

What This Book Was Actually For

This book was not primarily about learning to say no. Saying no is a skill. Skills can be learned in an afternoon.

This book was about something harder and more important: learning to believe that you matter enough to protect.

That your time matters. That your energy matters. That your peace matters. That the version of you that shows up when you are not performing and managing and accommodating, that version matters and deserves to exist in the world without constant justification.

That belief, however fragile, however contested by the old voices, however long it takes to settle into your bones, is what every tool in this book was designed to serve. The scripts and the strategies are in service of the belief. The belief is the thing.

And the belief, once you have it, really have it, not just understand it intellectually but feel it in the quiet moments when no one is asking anything of you, changes everything. Not dramatically. Not all at once. But consistently, in the direction of a life that is actually yours.

The Work Continues

You will put this book down and return to your life. And your life will present you with the same situations, the same people, the same pressures and patterns and moments of choice that it always has.

The difference is that you now have more. More language. More understanding. More tools. More evidence, from whatever work you have already done, that you are capable of something different.

It will not always be enough. There will be days when you know everything in this book and still cannot make yourself use it. Days when the guilt is louder than the clarity, when the old pattern wins, and when you end up back where you started and wonder if anything has actually changed.

On those days, come back. To this book, to your blueprint, and to the part of you that started this work because something in your life had to change. That part of you is still there. It has not abandoned you on the hard days. It is waiting for you to return to it.

The work is not finished when you finish this book. It is ongoing, for months, for years, possibly for the rest of your life. Not because you are broken and require constant repair, but because becoming more fully yourself is a lifelong project, and this is one chapter of it.

Some of what you have read will stay with you immediately. Some will take time to land. Some ideas will sit dormant for months and then surface in a moment when you need them, not as something you remember reading but as something you simply know.

That is how this kind of learning works. It does not happen all at once. It happens in layers, each practice and each difficult moment that you navigate a little better than the last, adding another layer to what you understand and who you are becoming.

You will have days when you hold every limit clearly and feel genuinely proud of who you are becoming. You will have days when the old patterns are louder than everything you have learned and you give in to something you swore you would not. Both kinds of days are part of this.

What you do on the second kind of day matters more than what you do on the first. The first kind of day is easy. The second kind is where the real work lives.

The people who change, the ones who actually build the life they want, who actually become someone with genuine limits and genuine presence, are not the ones who only show up on the easy days. They are the ones who show up on the hard ones too.

A Final Note on Imperfection

You will not do this perfectly. You were never going to. Perfection was never the goal.

The goal was movement. Movement in the direction of a life where you are more present, more honest, more genuinely connected, and more yourself. Movement toward the version of you that has limits because they love themselves, not because they have learned the rules. Movement toward relationships that nourish you, work you find meaningful, and days that feel like they belong to you.

That movement does not require perfection. It requires honesty about where you are, willingness to keep going, and the refusal to let the gap between who you are now and who you are becoming be a reason to stop.

You are not too far gone. You are not too old. You are not too deeply wired for this to change. Whatever the old voices say about that, they are not telling the truth.

You are exactly where you are, which is somewhere in the middle of something that matters. And the fact that you read this book, that you are still here on the last page, is evidence of something real.

The people who pick up a book like this and actually read it to actually do something with it, not to feel good in the moment but to genuinely change something, are already doing something most people never do. They are deciding that their life, as it is, is not the final word. That something different is possible. That they are worth the effort of becoming more themselves.

You are one of those people. Whatever brought you here, whatever made you willing to look honestly at these patterns and sit with the discomfort of what you found, that willingness is a form of courage. Do not minimize it.

The Most Important Limit

If you take only one thing from this book, let it be this: the most important limit you will ever set is the one that says I am worth protecting.

Everything else follows from that.

The no's and the consequences and the conversations and the grief and the growth, all of it follows from the foundational decision that you matter enough to protect. That your life is worth designing intentionally. That the people in it should know you, the real you, and be there for that person.

That is not a small decision. For someone who has spent years communicating through their actions that everyone else's needs come before their own, it is one of the most radical decisions available. It does not require a dramatic announcement. It does not require a confrontation or a declaration. It simply requires, quietly, in the ordinary moments of ordinary days, choosing yourself. Not instead of the people you love, but alongside them.

You are allowed to be one of the people you take care of.

You are worth protecting.

You always were.

Now go live like you believe it.

Reflection Questions

What is the one idea from this book that has changed how you see yourself? How has it changed what you do?

Where have you already made progress, however small, in the work of this book? What is the evidence of that progress?

What is the most important limit you have not yet set? What is your plan for setting it?

Who is the person you are becoming? How is that person different from the one who started this book?

What do you want to remember about why you started this work, for the days when you forget?

Your Chapter 25 Practice

This week, write a letter to yourself. Not to the past self, that was Chapter 19. To the future self. The person you are working toward.

Tell that person what you are building. Tell them what you have learned. Tell them what you want for them, for the life ahead of them, for the relationships and the days and the ordinary moments that make up a life.

Then read it back. Notice how it feels to articulate what you are moving toward. Notice if it feels possible. Notice if it feels like yours.

It is yours. This work is yours. The life you are building is yours.

Go build it.

BONUS MATERIALS

Quick-Reference Scripts

These scripts are drawn from throughout the book. Use them as starting points and adjust the language to fit your voice and your situation.

Saying No: The Core Scripts

• "That doesn't work for me."

• "I'm not going to be able to do that."

• "I've already made my decision. My answer hasn't changed."

• "I understand you're disappointed. The answer is still no."

• "I'm not going to discuss this further."

When They Push Back

• "I hear you. My answer is still no."

• "I understand we see this differently. I'm not going to change my position."

• "I'm going to end this conversation now. We can talk another time."

• "That's not something I'm willing to negotiate."

Setting a Limit with a Consequence

• "When [behavior happens], I'm going to [specific action I will take]."

• "I've mentioned this before. If it happens again, I'm going to [consequence]."

• "I need you to hear this clearly. If this continues, I will [consequence]."

Family Scripts

• "I understand you're disappointed. I'm not able to make it."

• "That topic is off the table when we talk. If it comes up, I'm going to end the call."

• "I love you. I also need you to stop commenting on [topic]."

• "I've already made my decision. I hope you can respect that."

Work Scripts

• "I'd like to make sure I can do this well. I currently have [X, Y, Z]. Can we talk about priorities?"

• "I generally don't monitor messages after [time]. I'll get back to you first thing in the morning."

• "I'd like to finish my point." (Then continue speaking.)

• "I appreciate you looking for a middle ground. My answer is still no on this one."

Relationship Scripts

• "There's something I've been wanting to bring up. When [situation], I feel [feeling]."

• "I hear that you see it differently. My feelings are real to me and I need them to be taken seriously."

• "I'm going to need some time to myself. I'm not pulling away. I just need space to recharge."

• "I've noticed this pattern. If it continues, I'm going to need to [consequence]."

Gray Rock Scripts (for toxic or narcissistic people)

• "Okay." (No elaboration.)

- "I'm not going to get into that."
- "I've just been busy." (End of response.)
- "That's not something I'm going to discuss."

30 Journal Prompts for Boundary Work

Use one prompt per day, or return to the ones that feel most alive for you. Write without editing. Let the honest answer surface before the managed one.

What did I say yes to today that I meant to say no to? What stopped me?

What am I most resentful about right now? What limit would address that resentment?

Who in my life makes me feel most like myself? What is different about how I show up with them?

What would I do with my time this week if I weren't managing other people's feelings?

What limit have I been wanting to set for more than six months? What has kept me from setting it?

When did I last feel genuinely rested? What were the conditions? How long ago was it?

What is the guilt voice saying to me right now? Is it healthy guilt or false guilt?

Who taught me that having limits was dangerous? What did they do when I tried to have them?

What am I tolerating in one key relationship that I would never advise a friend to tolerate?

What would my life look like in one year if I held my three most important limits consistently?

What do I actually want, not what I think I should want, not what would make others happy, right now?

What have I been apologizing for that doesn't require an apology?

Where in my life am I performing strength or availability that I don't actually feel?

What relationship in my life gives back as much as I put in? How does that feel different?

What does the word “selfish” mean to me? Where did that definition come from? Is it accurate?

What limit did I hold this week, however small? What did it cost me? What did it give me?

When I imagine showing up as my full, honest self in [key relationship], what am I afraid would happen?

What is one thing I've been giving compulsively that I could choose to give instead, or not give at all?

Who am I becoming? Describe this person in three sentences.

What does genuine belonging feel like in my body? When did I last feel it?

What consequence have I stated but not followed through on? What would change if I followed through?

What is the one limit that, if I held it consistently, would change the most about my daily life?

What am I carrying that isn't mine to carry? Where did I pick it up?

If I treated myself the way I treat the people I most respect, what would be different?

What does the hardest conversation I've been avoiding need me to say? Write it out.

When I slip and give in to the old pattern, what do I say to myself afterward? What would be more useful?

What is one relationship I've been maintaining out of habit rather than genuine connection?

What would I stop doing tomorrow if I knew no one would be upset about it?

What am I most proud of in my limit work so far, however small?

What do I want to say to the version of myself that started this work? Write that letter.

People-Pleasing Quick-Reference Checklist

Use this checklist to identify active patterns. Check any that apply to your current experience.

Signs You May Be People-Pleasing Right Now:

- I agreed to something I didn't want to do to avoid conflict.
- I said "I'm fine" when I wasn't.
- I apologized for something that wasn't my fault.
- I changed my opinion to match someone else's.
- I've been monitoring someone's mood and adjusting my behavior to manage it.
- I stayed in a conversation past the point where I wanted to leave.
- I gave a reason for my "no" when I didn't owe one.
- I felt guilty for taking time for myself.
- I did something I resent doing, and didn't say so.
- I said "whatever you want" when I had a preference.

Signs Your Limit Work Is Taking Hold:

- I said no to something small without apologizing.

- I felt the guilt and held the limit anyway.
- I named what I was feeling, to myself or to someone else.
- I left a situation that wasn't working for me.
- I asked for something I needed.
- I let someone's disappointment be theirs to manage.
- I showed up as myself instead of who I thought they needed me to be.
- I followed through on a consequence.
- I kept a promise I made to myself.
- I took up space without justifying it.

Recommended Reading

These books have supported many people doing this work. They are offered as companions, not requirements.

On Boundaries and People-Pleasing:

- Set Boundaries, Find Peace by Nedra Tawwab
- The Disease to Please by Harriet B. Braiker
- Not Nice by Dr. Aziz Gazipura
- Codependent No More by Melody Beattie
- Where to Draw the Line by Anne Katherine

On Self-Worth and Self-Respect:

- The Six Pillars of Self-Esteem by Nathaniel Branden
- Self-Compassion by Dr. Kristin Neff
- The Gifts of Imperfection by Brené Brown
- Radical Acceptance by Tara Brach

On Narcissistic and Toxic Relationships:

- STOP! You May Be a Narcissist or Know One by Kim R. Toppin

- Why Does He Do That? by Lundy Bancroft
- Psychopath Free by Jackson MacKenzie
- Adult Children of Emotionally Immature Parents by Lindsay C. Gibson

On Communication and Relationships:

- Nonviolent Communication by Marshall B. Rosenberg
- Difficult Conversations by Stone, Patton, and Heen
- Hold Me Tight by Dr. Sue Johnson

A FINAL NOTE ON GETTING HELP

Reading a book about limits is a meaningful first step. Doing the work, consistently, over time, with the support of other people, is what makes those limits real.

If the patterns described in this book feel deeply entrenched, if the guilt is overwhelming, if you find yourself reading chapter after chapter and recognizing yourself but unable to change anything, please consider reaching out to a therapist.

Not because something is wrong with you. Because this work is genuinely difficult, and having a trained professional to support you through it can make an enormous difference. The right therapist, particularly one with experience in codependency, trauma, or narcissistic abuse recovery, can offer what no book can: a consistent, attuned relationship in which the work of changing your patterns actually happens in real time.

You deserve that kind of support. Seeking it is not weakness. It is one of the most powerful limits you can set on behalf of yourself, the limit that says I am worth investing in.

If you are in immediate danger or crisis, please call 988 or your local emergency services. You do not have to manage a crisis alone.

ABOUT THE AUTHOR

Kim R. Toppin is an author and advocate for emotional wellbeing whose work helps readers break the patterns that keep them from living authentically and fully as themselves.

Her debut book, STOP! You May Be a Narcissist or Know One, grew from a deeply personal reckoning with narcissistic behavior and its effects on relationships, identity, and self-worth. Written with unflinching honesty and compassion, it has helped readers around the world recognize toxic patterns, protect themselves, and begin the long work of healing. The book has become a trusted companion for survivors of narcissistic relationships seeking language for what they experienced and a path forward.

Boundaries Without Guilt: How to Stop People-Pleasing, Set Firm Limits, and Take Back Your Power is the natural companion to that first book, the next step for readers who have recognized the patterns and are ready to change them. Where STOP! illuminated the problem, Boundaries Without Guilt provides the tools: the language, the frameworks, the scripts, and the self-respect practices that make genuine change possible over time.

Together, the two books form a complete roadmap for anyone who has spent too long absorbing what they should not, giving more than they have, and making themselves smaller to keep someone else comfortable.

Kim writes from experience, not from a position of having it all figured out, but from the ongoing, imperfect, worthwhile work of becoming someone who shows up honestly. Her voice is direct, warm, and grounded in the conviction that the people who most need these tools are often the last to believe they deserve them.

She lives in Maryland and continues to write about emotional health, self-respect, and the quiet courage it takes to take your own life seriously.

Also by Kim R. Toppin

STOP! You May Be a Narcissist or Know One

Available on Amazon and Kindle

www.ingramcontent.com/pod-product-compliance
Lightning Source LLC
LaVergne TN
LVHW020717110826
845149LV00012B/2307

* 9 7 9 8 9 9 4 0 8 6 2 7 8 *